Ginger glanced at the bookshelf. Something was different . . . rearranged. Her doll collection? There was the wooden shoe doll from Holland, the African doll, the—Where was the Japanese doll? The one in a kimona?

Her mind flashed to how awkwardly Robin had carried her windbreaker as she left. Had she hidden the doll under it? No one else had been in her room. But why would Robin do such an awful thing?

Lord, how can I love my neighbor, Ginger asked, *if my neighbor steals my stuff?*

The Ginger Series
by Elaine L. Schulte

Here Comes Ginger!
Off to a New Start
A Job for an Angel
Absolutely Green
Go For It!

A JOB FOR AN ANGEL

Elaine L. Schulte

Chariot Books™
David C. Cook Publishing Co.

A White Horse Book
Published by Chariot Books,™
an imprint of David C. Cook Publishing Co.
David C. Cook Publishing Co., Elgin, Illinois
David C. Cook Publishing Co., Weston, Ontario

A JOB FOR AN ANGEL
© 1989 by Elaine L. Schulte

The quotation on page 23 is from *The Wind in the Willows* by
Kenneth Grahame, published by Charles Scribner's Sons.

All Scripture quotations in this publication are from the Holy
Bible, New International Version. Copyright © 1973, 1978, 1984,
International Bible Society.

Cover design by Ad/Plus, Ltd.
Cover illustration by Janice Skivington
First printing, 1989
Printed in the United States of America
98 97 96 95 94   10 9 8 7 6 5 4

Library of Congress Cataloging-in-Publication Data

Schulte, Elaine, L.
  A job for an angel / Elaine L. Schulte.
    p. cm.—(A Ginger book)
  Summary: Ginger finds it hard to follow the commandment "Love your
neighbor as yourself" when troublemaker Robin enrolls in Ginger's
Christian school.
  ISBN 1-55513-782-2
  [1. Schools—Fiction. 2. Christian life—Fiction.]   I. Title
II. Series: Schulte, Elaine L. Ginger book.
PZ7.S3867Jo 1989
[Fic.]—dc19   88-35037
                                                              CIP
                                                              AC

*To Alex,
with a heart
full of love*

1

Ginger shoved a stick of gum into her mouth and shot the crunched wrapper into her wastebasket. She'd wear her green dress, she decided. She chewed faster and faster, trying to wake up, and a strange feeling hit. It was going to be a weird day.

An hour later in her fifth-grade classroom, she felt sure of the day's weirdness. She'd no more than stuck her gum under her desk than Miss Nordstrom stepped into the room with a new girl and looked straight at Ginger.

"Class, I'd like you to meet our new student, Robin Lindberg," Miss Nordstrom said. "Robin moved here from New Orleans, Louisiana, and I hope you'll all make her feel welcome—especially you, Ginger. I'd like you to be her buddy."

"Me? You want *me* to be her buddy?" Ginger asked. She'd only attended Santa Rosita Christian since the school year started in September, just one month ago.

Miss Nordstrom smiled. "I can't think of anyone more suited to the job. You've recently learned your way around school, so you're aware of everything a new student needs to learn. And, of course, you know about our buddy system for new students during their first few weeks of school."

"Sure . . . I mean, yes, ma'am," Ginger replied.

Ginger glanced at the new girl. With a name like Robin, Ginger thought, the girl should look cheerful, but she didn't. Dirty blonde hair hung over her pale cheeks like a dingy curtain, half hiding her grouchy face. Her plain blackish-blue dress didn't help. Instead of being cheery, she looked like a gray cloud coming to darken all of them.

Ginger forced a smile at her, but Robin just scowled.

Miss Nordstrom said to the kids sitting near Ginger, "Let's move this empty desk for Robin beside Ginger's. I start the school year with everyone sitting in alphabetical order, but that soon ends." She turned to Robin. "I understand you'll ride to school with Ginger, too."

"I guess so," Robin answered, still glum.

Since when? Ginger wondered.

While desks were being shoved all around them,

8

she remembered. Old Mrs. Lindberg down the street had a great-granddaughter from New Orleans moving in with her. This must be the one.

"Hi," Ginger said as Robin sat down next to her.

"Hi, yourself!" Robin shot back in a nasty tone.

Ginger swallowed hard and turned toward the front of the room.

Up front, Miss Nordstrom said, "Let's start our school day with prayer."

Good thing, Ginger thought. *I'm going to need it.*

As the prayer ended, she began to remember more. Drugs . . . yes, that was it. Robin's parents were in jail in New Orleans because of selling drugs, so she'd had to come live with old Mrs. Lindberg. Ginger felt her heart melt a little. Maybe she'd try to help Robin.

Ginger glanced at her again. She might even be pretty if she lightened up. With her blue eyes and dark blonde hair, she could look lots better than a girl with green eyes, wild red curls, and freckles— like one Ginger Trumbell.

"What are you gawking at me for?" Robin demanded.

Half the class turned toward them.

"Sorry," Ginger whispered, her cheeks getting hot. She pretended nothing was wrong and stared blindly at the blackboard.

The next time she looked, she caught Robin fooling with her hair in front of her neck. It looked as if she meant to strangle herself.

9

Finally it was time for morning recess. On their way outdoors, Ginger spoke to Robin as nicely as she could. "You want to play soccer with us?"

Robin's eyes narrowed. "I hate sports, and I hate goody-goodies like you, and I hate being in a Christian school!"

Ufffff! Ginger thought, letting out her breath. When she recovered, she said, "I'll show you where the rest room is."

Anne-Marie Walters passed by. "I can't wait until your birthday outing tomorrow, Ginger!"

"Me either," Lora Huckstep called over. "I love the San Diego Wild Animal Park!"

Ginger brightened. "I almost forgot!"

Beside her, Robin turned with interest, but Ginger didn't feel like explaining. Instead, she began to introduce her to their classmates. "Robin, this is—"

"Never mind!" Robin snapped and hurried off toward the rest room, hunched up in her dark dress.

"What's wrong with her?" Anne-Marie asked.

Ginger shrugged. "I guess she feels strange here."

"I guess so!" Anne-Marie said, moving on.

"Hey, Ginger!" Katie Cameron called out, catching up with Ginger as she walked out to the playground. Katie was a cheerful sight in her yellow dress and matching yellow yarn that tied her straight brown hair into a ponytail. "Did you know Robin would be riding with us to school?"

"I didn't know anything about it."

10

"Does that mean she'll ride home with us every afternoon, too?" Katie asked. Ginger's new stepfather, Grant Gabriel, was principal of the high school, and he drove them to school mornings. Katie's mother picked them up afternoons.

"It sounds like it to me," Ginger said. "Maybe Mrs. Lindberg brought her this morning and asked about rides then."

"The office could have arranged it," Katie said, her southern voice soft and thoughtful. "Anyhow, Robin looks interesting."

"Yeah," Ginger agreed. "Interesting, but not much fun."

"Are you going to ask her to your birthday outing tomorrow?" Katie asked.

"I guess not! She said she hates goody-goodies like me, and she hates being in a Christian school."

"She said that?" Katie asked, her brown eyes sparkling. "You, a goody-goody?"

Ginger had to smile herself. "Yeah. That's what she called me. I couldn't believe it."

"Maybe she's not a Christian," Katie said. "Not everyone here is, even if it is a Christian school."

"She sure doesn't act like it," Ginger answered, "but I'm not so good at it yet myself. Anyhow, it was bad enough to have the flu on my birthday. I don't want the birthday outing ruined, too."

Katie looked unconvinced. "I can't blame you, but—"

"Yeah, I know," Ginger said. "All of the other

girls in the class are invited."

"We should be especially nice to her," Katie said.

"A girl like that would spoil everything!" Ginger protested as they stood there in the warm sunshine. She didn't tell Katie an even meaner thought: maybe Robin Lindberg would be expelled from Santa Rosita Christian, since private schools didn't have to keep problem kids.

"Here she comes," Katie warned.

Robin approached them, still scowling. "Are you talking about me?" she asked.

Katie laughed. "Hey! How did you guess? I'm Katie Cameron. Welcome to Santa Rosita Christian . . . and welcome to our neighborhood. I hope we'll be friends."

"I'll bet," Robin answered.

Things didn't change much with Robin all day, even on the way home in Katie's mother's car. They all tried to be kind to her, including Mrs. Cameron, whose Georgia accent usually charmed everyone.

"What a pleasure to meet you," she said, and, "We'd surely be pleased to help y'all in any way, Robin. Let us know if there's anything we can do, heah?"

Robin, half-hidden by her curtain of hair, didn't answer. She seemed determined to be as grim as her blackish-blue dress.

For her part, Ginger felt just as determined to stay cheerful, so she kept her mind on the birthday outing coming the next day.

After Mrs. Cameron dropped her off, Ginger ran down the shady lane of eucalyptus trees toward the Gabriel house.

My house now, too, she reminded herself. She'd only lived there six weeks, since the beginning of September, but it was a welcoming sight. Purple bougainvillea bloomed against the white walls of the red tiled roof Spanish house, and red geraniums circled the green lawn.

She decided to put Robin out of mind. Anyway, Friday was the best day of the school week. For one thing, her sixth-grader stepbrother, Joshua, stayed late to work in the computer room. If her stepsister, Lilabet, was still napping, Mom wouldn't be busy with them.

Raffles, a shaggy gray-and-white blimp of a dog, ran from the front steps. "Woof!" he barked hoarsely. "Woof!"

"Woof yourself, Raffles!" Ginger called out with a laugh. She gave his shaggy head a good rub. "You love me, don't you, you old rascal? Even after my bad tricks."

Raffles wagged his tail-less rear end.

"Come on," she urged, no longer minding his doggy smell.

He panted beside her as they made their way through the sunshine to the side of the house.

Ginger opened the black iron gate and eyed the now familiar Gabriel sign. "Gabriel" was her step-family's name: Grant's, Joshua's, Lilabet's, and

13

Mom's now, too. There was also Grant's father, Grandfather Gabriel, a retired minister who lived in the guest house out back and was writing a book.

Grant said Gabriel was the name of an archangel, too, and he believed it. Ginger wasn't sure about that yet, but she believed in Jesus now, and her life had become better ever since. Just thinking about Him, joy bubbled in her heart. Maybe there was an angel gliding along with her now.

"Michael, row the boat ashore . . . hallelujah!" she sang out, feeling free and joyous. It hadn't been easy getting through her parents' divorce three years ago, and Mom marrying Grant Gabriel last summer, and moving into his house with them and his kids. *Thank You, Lord, for getting me through all of it,* she prayed, then was glad she'd remembered to thank Him.

"Michael, row the boat ashore!" she blasted out again as she opened the door to the family room. To her delight, the smell of freshly baked cookies filled the air.

"Well, don't you sound happy?" her mother called from the kitchen. She stood behind the counter chopping tomatoes, celery, and onions. "You know, Raffles wanted out the front door to wait for you about ten minutes ago. Somehow he knew you were due home."

"Good old dog," Ginger said, rubbing Raffles' head again.

Her mother nodded toward a plate of cookies on

14

the counter. "I don't suppose chocolate chip cookies would make you happier yet?" she asked.

Ginger plopped her blue denim book bag on a chair and grabbed two warm cookies. "Thanks! I am s-t-a-r-v-i-n-g!"

"I do love to hear you sing," her mother said, coming around the counter to give Ginger a kiss. Mom seemed to be in a just-the-two-of-us mood, which made her even more beautiful. As it was, she had dimples, blue eyes, a soft curvy shape, and wavy reddish-brown hair the shade of autumn leaves.

"You mean because my singing's so good?" Ginger teased.

"Nope," her mother returned. "Because I love to see you happy. I wish you could eat cookies and sing at the same time. Sit down and I'll get you a glass of milk. I'm making spaghetti for dinner."

Ginger stuck her gum under the kitchen counter as she sat down, then munched on a cookie. "Delicious!"

Her mother poured a tall glass of milk for her. "Thanks. How would you like to have a job?"

"Baby-sitting?" Ginger guessed, taking a drink of milk. Sometimes she baby-sat Lilabet now. It wasn't too bad taking care of a three-year-old if you watched her every minute.

"Not sitting with a child," Mom answered. "Visiting with Katie's great-aunt after school on Wednesdays. Her nurse has to leave at three, and you'd only have to stay for about two hours while

15

Mrs. Cameron takes Katie to piano lessons."

"Katie's mother didn't say anything about it on the way home," Ginger said.

"Because it's Mrs. Cameron, senior, who's doing the hiring," Mom explained. "She wanted to meet me first and see what I thought of the idea."

"But isn't she awfully sick?" Ginger asked. "Katie said she came in an ambulance with her nurse."

"Yes, she is sick, but Aunt Alice, as she prefers to be called, is better company than lots of people who are well."

Like Robin Lindberg, Ginger thought, then she felt mean for thinking it.

"How I'd love to paint a picture of Aunt Alice. She has the most beautiful sky blue eyes and such good bones, an aristocratic face. You know, noble and elegant," Mom explained. She'd started taking art classes, so she saw people and everything else differently—and she wasn't as tired as when she'd worked. Not that she didn't work hard at home, especially with four people, including a preschooler, to care for now.

Mom asked, "Do you think you'd like the job?"

"I don't know," Ginger answered uneasily.

"It might just be mid-October, but Christmas is only two months away," her mother said. "You wanted to make money for gifts this year."

"I sure do," Ginger agreed. Last year, she'd given Mom, Dad, and Gram cheap stuff. This year she wanted to give them nice presents, and now she'd

16

have to buy things for the Gabriels, too. "What would I have to do if I worked there?"

"Just keep her company. She likes to be read to because her eyes tire easily. I'll be right here, next door, if you need me. I'd go myself, but usually Lilabet's still napping then."

"Maybe I will," Ginger decided. She finished her milk, still feeling nervous about working for such a sick person.

"Why don't you go over right now?" Mom suggested. "She'd like to meet you and, of course, Katie's mother needs to know if arrangements are made. The pay is very good."

When she mentioned how much, Ginger exclaimed, "Guess I better go before someone else finds out about it!"

Her mother laughed. "Take Raffles along. She really liked him and Lilabet."

If this Aunt Alice liked Raffles and Lilabet, she couldn't be too bad, Ginger decided. "Okay. Come on, Raffles."

"Woof!" he answered.

As they started out the door, Ginger's mother called after them, "I saw Mrs. Lindberg at the supermarket this morning. Since all of the girls in your class are invited to your birthday outing tomorrow, I told her to invite her great-granddaughter, Robin, for us. She was eleven last month, so I assumed she was in your class and—"

"Robin Lindberg?!" Ginger interrupted in shock.

Her mother blinked. "I hope I did the right thing."

Ufffff! thought Ginger. Even if inviting Robin was the right thing to do, it didn't make her feel at all better.

Ufffff and *double ufffff* again.

2

"Come on, Raffles," Ginger urged as she set out from the Cameron house on her backyard shortcut. Why, oh, why did Mom invite Robin to go with them tomorrow? She'd ruin the whole day.

Approaching the wood-shingled, cream-colored house, she felt more unsure about sitting with a sick old lady, too. What if she got really sick while Ginger was there? What if she died on her? Undecided, Ginger stopped on the brick patio, Raffles panting and peering up at her curiously.

A woman's voice floated through the screen by the French doors. "You must be Ginger."

Trapped, Ginger thought. *Too late to escape.*

"I'm so glad you came around back," the woman

added cheerfully. "It seems ever so much more friendly, don't you think? Please come in."

Ginger opened the screen door uneasily.

"Wonderful! You've brought Raffles," the woman said. Her voice was soft, but not as southern as Katie's or her mother's.

"Yeah," Ginger answered, stepping into the bedroom.

"I'm delighted to see him again. I've always been fond of old English sheepdogs, although I do wish God had given them proper tails like other dogs."

Katie's great-aunt sat up in a hospital bed, books scattered over her blanket and potted chrysanthemums blooming around the sunlit room. "Katie calls me Aunt Alice," she said. "I hope you will, too."

"Thanks," Ginger answered.

She scrutinized the elderly woman. Her eyes were as blue as her ruffled bed jacket and, despite her wrinkles, her face had a joyous beauty. Her thick white hair was brushed back and curly at the edges, and she didn't just smile, she beamed. Her presence turned the bedroom into a lovely place.

"Are you a budding artist like your mother, and already sketching me in your mind's eye?" Aunt Alice inquired.

"Not me," Ginger said, blushing to be caught staring. "Mom told me you have 'sky blue eyes' and 'an aristocratic face,' and I decided that she was right. You really do."

"Why, thank you," Aunt Alice said. She began to smile again, then stopped as if she were in pain.

Ginger tensed.

The pain seemed to pass quickly, and Aunt Alice said, "Katie told me what fun you are. I've been eager to meet you." She settled back against her bed pillows. "How was school today?"

Ginger remembered Robin Lindberg. "Not so good."

"No? Why is that?"

"Miss Nordstrom gave me a new girl to show around."

"And . . . ?"

"She's the grouchiest girl I've ever seen."

"Hmmmm," Aunt Alice replied. "Sounds like guardian angel duty to me."

"I'm no angel!" Ginger protested. She quickly added, "I'm starting a collection of angels, though. Grandfather Gabriel gave me a carved wooden angel for my birthday."

"He told me that his late wife collected angels," Aunt Alice said. "A most suitable pursuit for anyone named Gabriel."

"You know him?" Ginger asked.

"Not the Angel Gabriel—yet," Aunt Alice answered with a laugh. "But I do know Grandfather Gabriel. He brought me that pot of yellow chrysanthemums the day after I arrived. As a matter of fact, he suggested you for my companion."

"He did? I thought it was Mom's idea."

"No, it was he who suggested you when I told him I needed someone," Aunt Alice answered. "He thinks highly of you, though I suspect he thinks the best of everyone."

"He does," Ginger agreed. "He gave me a book about angels, but it doesn't say much about the guardian kind. What do you think a guardian angel is anyway?"

"I expect there are two meanings to it," Aunt Alice answered. "Some people think a guardian angel is one who watches over and guards human beings. But it can mean anyone who helps another person, too, and that's what I expect you're to be, Ginger—a friend to your new classmate."

"Grandfather Gabriel has a picture of a guardian angel in his study," Ginger said, remembering. "It's of a girl walking through the woods and, right behind her, almost as tall as the trees' trunks, a beautiful angel glows with a heavenly light. The girl doesn't know the angel's behind her, but all of the deer, rabbits, birds, and squirrels in the woods know, and they've stopped everything to watch."

"It sounds beautiful," Aunt Alice said.

Ginger asked, "Should I ask him to bring it over?"

"If it's not too heavy, I'd enjoy that."

They smiled at each other, and Aunt Alice said, "I'd very much like to have you as my companion, Ginger. I need someone who'll visit and tell me about the outside world, since I can't get out. And I need someone who'll read, since my eyes are often too tired. Your mother tells me that you read well."

"I'm in the best reading group in school," Ginger answered, then wished it hadn't sounded boastful.

"Wonderful," Aunt Alice said and handed her a book. "Why don't you try reading from this?"

Ginger stared at the title: *The Wind in the Willows.* "A kids' book?"

Aunt Alice gave a laugh. "I think some of them are better than most adult novels nowadays. And *The Wind in the Willows* has great depth of feeling, don't you think?"

"I've never read it," Ginger admitted.

"Then we'll both be in for a treat," Aunt Alice said, lying back again. "Well, now, let's see if you enjoy it."

Ginger opened the book and began to read from the first chapter, "The River Bank."

The Mole had been working very hard all the morning, spring-cleaning his little home. First with brooms, then with dusters; then on ladders and steps and chairs, with a brush and a pail of whitewash; till he had dust in his throat and eyes, and splashes of whitewash all over his black fur, and an aching back and weary arms. Spring was moving in the air above and in the earth below and around him, penetrating even his dark and lowly little house with its spirit of divine discontent and longing. It was small wonder, then, that he suddenly flung his brush on the floor. . . .

As Ginger read on, she began to enjoy the story and to feel more comfortable. At length she finished the first chapter. "Is this all I'll have to do? Talk and read books?"

"You might have to fetch me a glass of water or other things, but mainly you'd read. Would you like to work for me on Wednesday afternoons?"

"I think I would," Ginger answered.

"Then you're hired to start next week," Aunt Alice said.

"Thanks, Aunt Alice! Thanks a lot!"

Maybe being a buddy to Robin Lindberg was awful, Ginger thought, but being a companion for Aunt Alice sounded as if it might be easy and even fun.

When Ginger arrived at home, the smell of simmering spaghetti sauce wafted from the kitchen. As if that weren't welcoming enough, Lilabet came running.

"Gin-ger!" she crowed. "Gin-ger!" Her brown eyes sparkled and her blonde hair shone as she threw herself into Ginger's arms.

"Hi, Lilabet," Ginger said and gave her a hug. Sometimes her little stepsister was a rascal like Raffles, but she was funny. The other day she'd said, "I got brown eyes from eating choc-lit, and I got yellow hair from eating ba-nanas." You never knew what she might say next, but you could count on her to get into trouble.

"You got shells for me?" Lilabet asked.

"I was at school today, not at the beach," Ginger replied.

"Oh," Lilabet answered, then she brightened. "We went shop-ping. We got choc-lit chips and toi-let paper, and we saw Miz Lind-berg."

"So I hear," Ginger answered unhappily.

Lilabet added, "Miz Lind-berg got a bird, Robin."

Mom had just come in from the hall, and she laughed. "Lilabet, I'm afraid I didn't explain that very well. Mrs. Lindberg has a great-granddaughter named Robin. And there are also birds named robins."

Lilabet scrunched up her face, confused.

"You'll see tomorrow," Mom said. "Robin will be along for Ginger's birthday outing. Robin Lindberg is a girl."

Unfortunately! Ginger thought.

Mom asked, "Would you two please set the table? Grandfather Gabriel is eating with us tonight, so be sure to set an extra place. We'll need salad plates, too, and dinner plates for the spaghetti and garlic bread."

Lilabet said, "I'll get nap-kins."

At least that kept her busy, Ginger thought, even though Lilabet only brought one napkin at a time to the table, and it took her forever. Ginger grabbed the new pottery dishes from the cabinet and began to set the table.

She was glad the dishes were a wedding present; sometimes she felt strange using things that had belonged to Grant's first wife. Anyhow, white dishes edged with clay-colored flowers looked perfect with the family room's Mexican tile floor. And, to go with the dishes, Mom had begun to stencil matching flowers around the kitchen ceiling.

Grant arrived at five-thirty. "Hello, everyone!"

Lilabet ran to him, calling, "Dad-dy, Dad-dy!" He caught her for a kiss, then swooped her up to the ceiling.

Ginger felt momentarily jealous. If only it were her father coming home! Yet she was glad it wasn't, too. Her feelings about Dad and the divorce were still a bad tangle. One good thing now, though—Mom was happy.

Before Ginger had time to think further about it, Grant gave her a hug. "Did you have a good day?" he asked, his grayish-blue eyes interested.

"It was okay," she responded.

Mom arrived from the laundry room with an armful of dried towels. "You're home!" she called out delightedly to Grant.

"There you are," he replied and headed for her. "I'm spending far too much of my day thinking about you."

Mom laughed. "I'm glad. I think about you all day, too."

Grant grabbed Mom, towels and all, and gave her a great big kiss.

It was too e-m-b-a-r-r-a-s-s-i-n-g, Ginger thought, but sort of good, since they were still newlyweds. Besides, it was better than fights, like Mom and Dad had before the divorce.

Lilabet asked, "Where's Josh-wa?"

Grant said, "He was putting things away in the garage. Here he comes now."

Probably Joshua was just trying not to be there to see the welcome-home kiss, Ginger thought. He still remembered his mother before she was killed in the freeway accident. Last night when Grant had kissed Mom, Joshua had mumbled something about "all that mush."

Lilabet yelled and ran so hard for Joshua that he had to grin. He had brown eyes and brown hair that was cut like Lilabet's: straight and sort of a bowl shape with bangs, only very nicely done. Lilabet reached up for a kiss from him, and Joshua turned to Ginger to ask, "What are you watching?"

"Not you!" Ginger answered. She grabbed her book bag. "I'm going to my room to wash up."

Joshua had been more pleasant before the wedding, Ginger thought. Ever since she and Mom moved in, he'd acted strange. Maybe he was jealous, because Grant, Lilabet, and Grandfather Gabriel spent lots of time with her. Maybe she should be kinder to him.

Later, when she returned, Grandfather was already there. "Happy birthday, Ginger," he said, handing her a pot of yellow chrysanthemums like the ones he'd given to Aunt Alice.

"Another present!" she said.

He grinned. "I thought we'd draw out your birthday a little longer. Besides, tomorrow is the big outing."

"Yeah," Ginger said. "Anyhow, nobody's ever given me flowers before. Thanks."

Grandfather Gabriel's eyes, grayish-blue eyes like Grant's, sparkled with pleasure. "Then I'm doubly pleased to have given them to you." The sun glinted in through the windows, making his silvery hair shine.

Ginger put the flowers on the table. It felt nice to share flowers with the family, even with Joshua.

When dinner was ready, Grant brought the spaghetti and garlic bread, and Joshua poured milk while Mom tossed the salad. Finally they sat down, Mom helping Lilabet into her booster chair. When they were settled, Grant said, "Let's sing the doxology today."

Ginger held hands with him and Grandfather, and they sang,

"Praise God from whom all blessings flow,
Praise Him all creatures here below,
Praise Him above, Ye heavenly host,
Praise Father, Son, and Holy Ghost."

As their harmonious "Amen" filled the room, Ginger felt at one with them, like part of the family.

Grandfather said to her, "I stopped by to visit Katie's great-aunt on the way here. I understand you're going to be her companion on Wednesday afternoons."

Ginger nodded, passing him the tossed salad.

He added, "It sounds like you've acquired two jobs today. She tells me Robin Lindberg is your buddy at school."

"Yeah," Ginger replied.

Mom said, "Ginger, you didn't tell me. I'm so grateful I invited Robin to join us for your birthday outing."

Ginger was glad the bowl of spaghetti had just come to her, and she helped herself to four big steaming spoonfuls without looking at them.

As if Robin coming to the birthday outing weren't bad enough, Joshua spoke up from across the table. "You must be crazy to work for Katie's great-aunt, Ginger. For one thing, I thought you wanted to play in the pickup soccer games at school Wednesdays. For another, everyone knows that Katie's great-aunt isn't going to live."

"Joshua, that's not compassionate," Grant said.

"Well, it's honest," Joshua returned.

Ginger scarcely heard the rest of their conversation. How could she have forgotten about soccer games on Wednesdays? And on top of that, Joshua was right—why had she ever agreed to work for someone who wasn't going to live?

3

"We're here! We're here!" the girls yelled as Ginger's mother parked the car in the San Diego Wild Animal Park lot.

Ginger spotted the van Grant had borrowed so the others could ride comfortably, too. "Here come the rest of them!"

Finally, her birthday outing! Every girl in the class had come except Julie, who had the flu. Even Robin Lindberg didn't look too glum, though she wore a dark top and jeans. The other girls wore bright, fun clothes like Ginger's bright green blouse and shorts that Gram had made.

"Everybody out," Ginger's mother said with a smile. She sounded excited, too.

They piled out and joined the other girls and Grant. "I don't know if I'm up to escorting this many girls," he laughed.

"We'd better be good," Katie joked. "He'll be our principal when we're in high school."

"Not mine," Robin Lindberg announced importantly. "I'll be gone by then. I'm going to acting school."

Ginger and Katie exchanged glances before Ginger said, "I didn't know you wanted to be an actress."

Robin's chin rose. "I'm one already."

Ginger didn't believe her. She turned to the others. "Come on, let's go!"

Walking up from the parking lot, she eyed the African buildings at the park entry. She hadn't been here since Mom's divorce, and no one was going to spoil this day for her, not even Robin Lindberg.

It took only minutes for tickets and the turnstiles, then they bumped through sets of wire mesh doors into the screened aviary. "Hey, it's jungly!" Katie exclaimed.

Tropical birds flew freely through the dense plants. Ginger pointed at a bright red and green parrot perched on a tree limb. "Look at that bird!"

Undaunted, the bird stared back at her, and Cassie Davis teased, "He's in love with Ginger's red hair!"

Ginger laughed merrily with the rest of them.

As they made their way through the aviary, exotic

31

birds twittered, tweeted, and cooed among ferns, vines, and trees. Ginger led the way over a rustic bridge, and a waterfall rushed under them to a small pond, making the lush setting even more beautiful. At the end of the aviary, she pushed through two other sets of wire mesh doors.

She blinked as they stepped out into the bright sunlight. On one side, a flock of pink flamingos posed on their stilty legs in front of a lagoon. Before her, flowers and trees surrounded exotic thatch-roofed huts and exhibits, and brightly dressed visitors spilled from a nearby amphitheater.

Grant suggested, "Let's have a picture of all of you sitting on the rhino."

"All right!" someone yelled.

They climbed up on a huge brass rhinocerous, the metal hot from the sun.

"Isn't this cool!" Cassie Davis yelled.

"Cool?" they repeated, laughing, for the metal almost burned their legs. They struck funny poses for the camera.

Mom suggested, "Let's start for the Congo River Fishing Village. There's time to see it on the way to the bird show."

"Let's go!" they answered.

Built of rustic poles, stick fences, and thatched roofs, the fishing village was wonderfully pictur-esque. Once there, they hurried up wooden cat-walks and looked down at the rushing river, where native fish traps lay near the rapids. In the distance,

African-style gift shops and restaurants beckoned, making it all seem more foreign.

"It's as if we're on a faraway trip," Ginger said. She thought everything would be perfect if Robin Lindberg didn't trail so far behind them. An awful idea hit. Robin's parents were in jail for dealing drugs. What if Robin was looking for drugs? No . . . it didn't seem possible.

Mom must have noticed her concern, for she said, "I'll keep Robin company."

"Thanks, Mom," Ginger said.

They stopped by Gorilla Grotto to make faces at the gorillas, and Ginger slowly began to forget her concern about Robin. After a while, it was time to wander on to the bird show.

Ginger vaguely remembered it as they entered the outdoor amphitheater. Huge green sunscreens shaded the audience on the half circle of bleachers; in front, a hedge enclosed the lawn and the tan cliffs that served as a stage. They settled halfway up the bleachers—Katie on one side of Ginger, Robin Lindberg on the other. Mom sat beside Robin on the aisle.

Mom called to Grant, "Do you have a dollar bill? Last time, they had a bird fly right to someone's hand for a bill. They called on volunteers by the aisle."

Grant dug out a crisp dollar bill and passed it up the row to her. "Just so the bird doesn't fly off with you," he joked.

Smiling, Mom tucked the bill into the sleeve pocket of her turquoise-colored blouse, next to Robin.

Music swirled through the amphitheater. Sky music, Ginger thought as a cloud of birds burst into the sky just above them, whirling and twirling. The birds somersaulted in midair, whipping about and doing backward flips. Ginger ooohed and ahhhed with the crowd, and asked Robin, "Isn't this wonderful?"

Robin mumbled, "It's okay."

Minutes later, even Robin looked awed as a huge blue and green parrot swooped past, circling low over the audience again and again. "Ladies and gentlemen," the announcer shouted as he ran onstage, "welcome to the Free-Flying Bird Show!"

The music crested again and again as a rose-breasted cockatoo flew over the delighted audience into overhead hoops.

Next, the announcer said, "We need a volunteer with a one-dollar bill."

Everywhere people waved their hands and dollar bills. Mom stood and waved her hand with them.

The announcer said, "The lady in the middle, the one wearing the turquoise blouse."

"Yeah, Mom!" Ginger yelled.

The announcer asked, "Do you have a dollar?"

"Right here in my sleeve pocket," Mom answered excitedly, fumbling for it. "Now where is it?"

Her smile slowly faded, replaced by dismay. "I'm sorry, I must have dropped it."

The announcer said, "That's too bad. Anyone else with a dollar bill?"

Ginger's mother sat down, searching around her. To Ginger's amazement, Robin jumped up and waved a crisp green dollar. "I do! Right here!"

"There," the announcer said, "the girl in dark blue. Now if you'd stand out by the aisle, and fold the dollar in half, then in half again until you have a square."

Ginger stared at her suspiciously. How did Mom's dollar disappear from her blouse sleeve pocket? . . . and how did Robin happen to have a crisp bill in her hand? She hadn't taken out a wallet or anything from her pockets.

A moment later, a rose-breasted cockatoo flew up to take the dollar from Robin's hand, then flew it to the announcer who joked, "Thank you so much," and pretended to keep it.

Everyone laughed, then finally the bird flew the dollar back to Robin, who smiled widely.

"All right, Robin!" Katie called out across Ginger.

"Good job, Robin!" Ginger's mother echoed with the others.

Ginger could only force a stiff smile at Robin as she sat back down, exultant.

The show continued with eagles, owls, a raven, and a hawk, but wonderful as it was, Ginger couldn't shake the idea that Robin had taken Mom's dollar.

After the bird show ended, they trooped out and

stopped at the nearby Hawk Talk, then visited Nairobi Village shops and the Petting Kraal, where they petted deer and goats.

A goat began to chew on Mom's straw purse and she joked, "I'd better get out of here! In any event, I wanted to do some shopping, then Grant and I will get the birthday cake and things. Here's the monorail tickets and a map, Ginger. We'll meet you at the Savannah Picnic Grove."

When everyone had finished admiring and petting the animals, Ginger announced to her classmates, "This way to the monorail!"

Ten minutes later, they rode the Wgasa Bush Line monorail through the wilderness, and Ginger watched animals graze on the grassy plains and hillsides, forgetting her suspicions about Robin. In the Eastern Africa exhibit, antelope, impala, and waterbuck roamed with Cape buffalo, rhino, gnu, and giraffes.

"It's awesome," Katie said.

While the monorail glided through the vast tan and green landscape, the driver told about the animals. Exotic deer, gazelle, antelope, and rhinos roamed the Asian Plains. The monorail passed through Northern Africa and Southern Africa plains, and everyone marveled at zebras, ostriches, and springbok. Other areas held tigers, elephants, and wild horses.

It was nearly an hour later when they climbed off the monorail. "I wish we could go again," Ginger said, "but we'd better start for the picnic grove."

They headed down the Kilimanjaro Trail, passing by elephants and cheetahs, then saw Grant coming for them. "We're all set for the birthday girl," he said.

"Happy birthday to you!" her friends sang out crazily, trooping to the picnic grove with her, grinning as other park visitors smiled at them. "Happy birthday to you. . . ."

Seated at a picnic table, they sang it properly over the birthday cake. Eleven green candles flickered in the warm breeze over the chocolate-frosted cake. Green icing under the candles spelled out, "Happy Birthday, Ginger!"

When they finished with "Many more birthdays to you," she took a deep breath to blow out the candles.

"Make a wish . . . make a wish," Katie reminded her.

Ginger thought, *I wish for all of us to have a perfect day, even Robin Lindberg.* She blew all of the candles out with one breath. Pleased, she looked up only to see that Robin had sunken back into sullenness.

Katie said, "I surely wish you could open your presents again, but it was better for you to have them on your real birthday. We wanted you to know we cared when you were sick."

"Right," Anne-Marie agreed.

"I might give you a present later," Robin said,

twisting her hair around in front of her neck again.

"Oh," Ginger answered, unsure what to say.

Minutes later, they sat eating the cake and drinking their soft drinks. It was a perfect place for a birthday party. Ginger looked at Mom, Grant, and her classmates. "This is the best birthday of my life. The very best."

Later, when they were seated in the bleachers for the elephant show, Ginger told Cassie, "I think they call for volunteers here, too. I'd sure like to be one of them."

Cassie said, "I'll yell that it's your birthday!"

"Okay," Ginger agreed.

She turned to study the stage just in case. A tan cliff rose behind leafy bamboo and palm trees. Beside the greenery, two elephant-sized green canvas curtains said, *San Diego Wild Animal Park*. The stage itself was hard sand, separated from the audience by a moat and a low fence.

Suddenly music filled the air and an announcer ran out. "Good afternoon . . . and welcome to the Elephant Show!" he shouted. "How is everyone doing today?"

The audience replied in a jumble of voices and applause.

"Where's everyone from?" he asked.

"Illinois!" someone shouted. "Canada!" "Massachusetts!"

Ginger waited excitedly, then finally heard: "We need some volunteers for our show today. A girl and a boy between eight and eleven, each with a parent. . . ."

She jumped up, waving both hands.

Cassie yelled, "It's her birthday!"

Ginger couldn't believe it, but there was Robin standing up in the row in front of them, waving her hands wildly, too.

The announcer said, "The girl in the green blouse and shorts . . . the birthday girl. Be sure to bring your mother down here with you."

"Come on, Mom," Ginger shouted, grabbing her mother's arm.

As Ginger passed by, Robin muttered, "You could have let me go. It's my birthday, too."

"Your birthday?" Ginger repeated.

Robin snapped, "Never mind!"

Robin had to be lying, Ginger thought as she headed down the stairs. Besides, Mom said Robin was eleven last month.

Ginger still felt shaken when they arrived by the stage.

The announcer asked their first names and ages, and Ginger answered nervously, "Ginger. I'm eleven."

Her mother replied with a smile, "My name is Sallie, and I'm not telling my age!"

The audience chuckled, and the announcer turned to introduce the boy volunteer, Jason, who was nine, and his father.

A park employee took them aside. "Wait here,

please," he said, and they stood by a small bridge to the stage. By the time Ginger looked up, two huge elephants plodded onstage, one ridden by a man, the other by a woman.

The announcer introduced the elephants and explained, "The riders are called *mahouts*. They usually meet their elephants at an early age, then spend the rest of their lives with them."

A mahout. That's what I'd like to be! Ginger thought, beginning to recapture her excitement.

She applauded with the audience as the elephants picked up small logs and dropped them into cargo boxes on the sandy stage. Nita, one of the elephants, rolled a huge log across the stage with her trunk.

After a while the announcer said, "And now we'll need our volunteers to help with relays."

Moments later, Ginger and her mother were on one side of the stage with the other volunteers; the elephants, ridden by their *mahouts*, were across from them. A row of blue bowling pins stretched between them, and she was supposed to get an apple from Mom's basket, zigzag through the bowling pins, and put the apple into Nita's trunk.

"Ready, set, go!" the announcer yelled.

Ginger grabbed an apple and zigzagged wildly through the row of bowling pins, then put the apple into Nita's trunk. While Nita ate it, Ginger tore back through the pins for another apple, then back and forth again. She heard the audience cheer and Mom yelled, "Faster, Ginger! Faster!" Finally Nita had the last apple, and Ginger raced back to touch Mom's hand.

"The winner is . . ." the announcer said, ". . . a tie."

The audience groaned because the announcer had helped Jason, but Ginger told her mother, "I know I won. It's only fun anyway."

"You *are* growing up," Mom replied proudly.

Next, the elephants had a relay, using their trunks to give the bowling pins to their *mahouts*.

"Nita wins again!" the announcer yelled.

After that came a race between Ginger and Jason to try to transfer apples like elephants do with their trunks. "Inhale each apple, then put it into the plastic cylinder," the announcer explained. "You can use one finger to help."

Ginger's apples fell to the ground, one after another. "This is impossible!" she laughed. She noticed Jason wasn't doing any better either.

"Nita wins again!" the announcer shouted.

As the audience laughed and applauded, the park employee escorted Ginger, Mom, Jason, and his father behind the stage backdrop. "Have you ever ridden an elephant?" he asked Ginger.

"No, never. . . ."

"We've got your elephant saddled," he said, nodding at the elephant. "Let's get you two up on her."

Before Ginger knew what had happened, she'd mounted the steps to a cargo box platform, then was climbing onto the elephant's huge saddle. She hung onto a bar while the *mahout* sat down in front of her and Jason behind her. Settled, she felt stunned while they waited to go onstage.

Mom said, "Hold on tightly. I hope Grant gets pictures!"

Out front, the announcer said something about the next act. Exciting music filled the air and, as the green canvas curtain opened, the *mahout* said to the elephant, "Move up, girl. Move up."

The elephant lumbered forward, the pads of its feet making *chh-a, chh-a, chh-a* sounds as they scraped against the hard sand. "And here they are!" the announcer shouted, "Let's hear some applause for our volunteers . . . Jason and Ginger!"

Ginger swayed slowly on the huge elephant's back, her heart thundering while the audience cheered. Katie and her other classmates stood on the other side of the moat and yelled, "Yea, Ginger! Yea, Ginger!"

Grant snapped picture after picture.

What a birthday! She never dreamed she'd ride an elephant! As they plodded forward, Ginger waved at her classmates, just barely hanging on.

"Yea, Ginger!" they yelled over and over. They looked as excited as she felt—all of them except one.

Ignoring Robin Lindberg's angry expression, Ginger waved again at the others. *I'm riding an elephant!* she thought. *I'm really and truly riding an elephant!* In the midst of such excitement, it seemed that nothing could ever go wrong again.

4

The next morning at Sunday school, Ginger felt ashamed of herself. Miss Tyler, their teacher, asked, "What is the Lord's second great commandment to us?"

Someone answered, "To love your neighbor as yourself."

"Who is your neighbor?" Miss Tyler asked.

It didn't take Ginger long to know that Robin Lindberg was her neighbor—and not just because she lived nearby. During the discussion, Ginger said, "It's hard to love some people."

The class agreed, and Miss Tyler said, "That's when we ask God to give us His love for them. We have to say, 'Lord, give me Your love for whoever-it-is.' We can't do it on our own."

43

Lord, give me Your love for Robin! Ginger prayed.

Miss Tyler asked, "Do you help your neighbor?"

Ginger recalled riding the elephant onstage yesterday. While the audience and all of her classmates except Robin had cheered, she'd done nothing to help Robin feel welcome. Instead, she'd selfishly thought about it being her birthday and having fun herself. The more she realized her selfishness, the more ashamed she felt.

On the way home she asked her mother, "Can I . . . I mean *may* I invite Katie and Robin Lindberg over this afternoon?"

Mom's dimples deepened. "I must say, you're full of surprises. Of course you may. You know, that gives me an idea. I'll invite Robin and Mrs. Lindberg for dinner. Why don't you call now, before lunch?"

"Okay." It did sound like a nice thing to do.

After lunch, Grandfather Gabriel drove Joshua somewhere, Lilabet was in bed for her afternoon nap, and Mom and Grant settled outside by the pool to read the Sunday newspapers.

At one-thirty, just when Katie and Robin were due, Katie phoned. "I can't come after all. I'm really sorry. Aunt Alice's cousins from Los Angeles stopped by to see her and us. Anyhow, I know you'll be fine with Robin."

"Yeah . . . and there's the doorbell already." Ginger gave her gum a disheartened crack. It would be a long afternoon playing with Robin until Mrs. Lindberg came at five o'clock.

When Ginger opened the door, Robin stood on the steps looking distrustful behind her curtain of hair. She wore dark clothes, as usual: jeans, blouse, and even a windbreaker, despite the warm day.

"Hi, Robin," Ginger said.

"Hi." Robin glanced around. "Is Katie here yet?"

"She just called. She can't come after all."

Robin's lips tightened. "I guess she doesn't like me."

"Why would you think that?" Ginger asked.

Robin shrugged uncertainly, still standing in the doorway.

"Katie likes everyone," Ginger told her. "Come on in. Maybe we can play a game or something in my room."

"Maybe we could act," Robin suggested.

"I don't know how," Ginger replied.

"It's easy, you just pretend," Robin said. "It's like being someone else . . . like being in a dream."

"I could try," Ginger decided and led the way to her room. With Robin's parents in jail, she probably liked to pretend she was someone else or maybe dreaming.

When they stepped into Ginger's room, Robin's eyes roved over every inch of the peach and white bedroom, lingering on the bookshelves around the window before moving down to the white fluffy rug. "It's a nice room," she said.

Ginger half apologized, "I'm usually not so neat. Katie helped me put my stuff away when I moved in."

She looked at everything anew herself. White chenille spreads covered the twin beds, and the bookshelves on the window wall were still amazingly neat. Her seashell collection sparkled, and books stood upright, separated by pictures, driftwood, rocks, and her globe; even the games were stacked. The top shelf held colorfully costumed dolls from around the world; another shelf held her stuffed animals, Spider, Octopus, Dinosaur, Fish, Fair Lion, and Parrot, who held the Bible verse card that began, "Put on the new self." Best of all she liked the carved wooden angel Grandfather had given her for her birthday.

"The window seat would make a good stage," Robin said. She took off her windbreaker and tossed it onto Ginger's bed.

"You think so?" Ginger asked.

Robin nodded. "I like your dolls from around the world. They've got good costumes."

Ginger eyed them. There were dolls from Holland, Africa, India, Japan, Costa Rica, Mexico, and other countries. "I don't mess with them much, maybe because I never had a place to put them out before. My grandparents from Virginia send them."

"Who's that in the picture?" Robin asked.

Ginger glanced at the picture. "My father."

"He's really handsome," Robin said.

Ginger tried to see the picture through Robin's eyes. Dad was tan, his white smile broad, and his dark hair curly.

"I heard he lives over by the beach," Robin said.

"Yeah. Yeah, he does." Ginger didn't want to explain about the divorce three years ago and the problems, like him not showing up to see her at Gram's house most Saturdays.

Suddenly Robin turned her back to her, hunching it up. A moment later, she turned with a beaming smile. "Who do you think I am now?"

Robin waved grandly as if to a crowd; her other hand gripped something as she rode along.

"I don't know anyone like that," Ginger answered.

Robin gave a snippy laugh. "Ginger Trumbell waving to the cheering crowd as she rides by on an elephant."

"Did I look that . . . pleased with myself?"

"You sure did," Robin answered. "Now, let's see if you know the next one." She turned her back, hunched up again, then turned. She smiled widely, then blew hard.

Ginger guessed, "Ginger Trumbell blowing out the candles on her birthday cake."

"You got it. Let's try another." This time when Robin turned back, she pretended to hold something up in one hand. With her other hand, she beckoned importantly for others to follow.

47

Ginger shook her head. "I don't know."

Robin said, "Ginger Trumbell announcing the way to the monorail at the Wild Animal Park."

"Was I really so . . . bossy?"

"What do you think?" Robin asked, and Ginger felt terrible. Robin added, "Why don't you act me out now?"

Feeling angry, Ginger considered being Robin during the bird show as she stole the dollar from Mom's sleeve pocket and then held it out for the bird . . . or staring up hatefully because she couldn't ride the elephant. Ashamed, she said, "I can't do it. I guess I don't know you well enough yet."

Robin sat down on the window seat like she owned it. "I could give you a pantomime to do."

"Okay," Ginger agreed reluctantly.

"You could be a movie nuisance," Robin suggested. "First, you shove ahead in the ticket line, then you get shoved back and wait. Next, you buy your ticket and drop the change and pick it up. Then you go in and buy popcorn. Spill some on the carpet and give it a kick. After that, you walk down the aisle and see a seat in the middle of a row. Crawl over lots of people, so everyone gets mad at you."

"I'll try it," Ginger decided. She turned around, then turning back, pretended to push ahead in a ticket line. She felt foolish, but she did it all anyhow.

"You could have swung your arms more and kicked the popcorn, really mad," Robin said. "You want to do a skit? We could write a skit and then act it."

"Okay," Ginger agreed. "Where did you learn how to do all of this stuff anyhow?"

"I got acting books from our library in New Orleans," Robin said, "then I'd act out the parts in front of the mirror."

"All of the parts?" Ginger asked.

"Sometimes when Mom was home, she'd do some of the others," Robin said, then looked like she wished she hadn't. She raised her chin. "Get a pencil and paper, and I'll think."

Ginger went to her scarred maple desk for a pencil and a half-used notebook. "How's this?"

Robin accepted it absentmindedly. "How about a story about an old woman and a tramp who comes to the door for food? She feeds him soup, then he ties her up and steals things."

Ginger asked, "You mean he wasn't even thankful? He stole everything, tied her up, and went away?"

"Why not?" Robin asked. "She's just an old woman."

"That's terrible," Ginger said. "I don't even want to be in a skit like that."

Robin asked in surprise, "How should it end?"

"The tramp would eat the soup and be grateful," Ginger decided. "Maybe he'd even offer to mow the lawn."

"Sounds dumb to me," Robin said.

49

Ginger countered, "I don't like it your way."

Robin's eyes met hers for an angry instant, then glanced down at the writing again. "All right, let's do it both ways."

Ginger agreed uneasily. It was weird to write about an old lady and a tramp, especially since Robin lived with her great-grandmother. Robin had arrived almost like a tramp herself . . . being taken in and fed. The idea bothered Ginger the whole time they wrote the skits and acted them out.

They'd just finished when Lilabet pounded on the door. "Can I come in, Gin-ger?" she asked. "Can I come in?"

Ginger said, "Sure, Lilabet, come on in."

Lilabet burst in, surprised to see Robin.

"Hi, Lilabet," Robin said. "You want to act, too?"

Lilabet answered uncertainly, "Okay."

"You can be Kitty," Robin said. "All you have to do is get down on your hands and knees like a cat and meow. The first one of us who laughs when you meow has to be Kitty next."

Lilabet frowned and Ginger explained again. Finally Lilabet understood. She got down on her hands and knees and gave a really strange, "Meee-owwww!"

Lilabet looked so peculiar, Ginger couldn't help laughing.

"Ginger is Kitty next," Robin announced as if she enjoyed being in charge.

With Lilabet playing with them, it was more fun,

Ginger decided. After Kitty, they played Statues and other acting games. Ginger wondered if Robin had played them with kids . . . or had she learned all of them from books?

After a while Lilabet asked, "Can we watch *Mary Poppins*?"

Ginger explained, "She has it on videotape." Then she said to Lilabet, "Robin and I are too old for *Mary Poppins*."

"I like to watch the acting," Robin said.

They settled on the family room carpet to watch the video, and Ginger felt relieved at not having to entertain Robin. It seemed that she liked acting and not much else.

When *Mary Poppins* ended, Joshua came home with Grandfather Gabriel, who drove off to get Mrs. Lindberg. She didn't like to drive. At least an end to Robin's visit was in sight, Ginger thought.

Before long, Grandfather Gabriel arrived with tiny Mrs. Lindberg. Her hair was white and wavy, but she was as spry and cheery as Ginger remembered. "It's so kind of you to invite us today," Mrs. Lindberg said in a loud voice. "My, Robin, you look like you've been having a fine time."

Robin shot her a disgusted glance, but Mrs. Lindberg was busy introducing her to Grandfather Gabriel.

"He used to be the pastor at my church, but he retired on us," she explained to Robin. "It just hasn't been the same since."

"It's a pleasure to meet you, Robin," Grandfather said.

Robin said a cold, "Hi," and eyed him suspiciously.

Mom said, "It's still such nice weather, we thought we could eat outside at the patio table. Can I get you girls to set it? I'll put the dishes on the kitchen window shelf."

"Sure," Ginger said, glad to be busy. It wasn't easy to "love your neighbor" when the neighbor was Robin Lindberg, but at least the afternoon hadn't been too terrible.

At six o'clock, when they sat down at the table and held hands as Grandfather said grace, Robin's hand felt all stiff and jerky and damp. When they'd finished, Ginger added silently, *Lord, help me love this neighbor as myself!*

Everything went well during dinner. Mrs. Lindberg pronounced Mom's chicken casserole "The best I've ever eaten in my life . . . and, at my age, that's a real compliment. Now when I lived in Texas, we fried our chicken—"

Robin muttered to Ginger, "She talks and talks and talks."

Listening to Mrs. Lindberg, it did seem that she talked a lot more than she listened. She even talked more than she ate. Ginger's mind returned to the skit. Mrs. Lindberg might talk loudly and a lot, but she didn't seem so bad that a tramp—or anyone else—should tie her up and steal her things.

After cookies and chocolate ice cream, Mrs. Lindberg said, "I do wish we could visit longer, but I tire easily these days. If you'd excuse us—"

Robin stood up from the table abruptly. "I'll be right back." She hurried from the table and into the house.

Ginger started after her, but Robin was already rushing down the hallway. "I can find the bathroom myself!" she snapped.

"Sorry!" Ginger replied, embarrassed, and returned outside.

After a while, Robin came out holding her windbreaker awkwardly, waiting as Mrs. Lindberg bid everyone a lengthy good-bye. She turned to Robin and asked loudly, "Aren't you going to thank Ginger and the Gabriels for a nice day?"

"Thanks for a nice day," Robin said, avoiding their eyes. She didn't even look at them as they got into Grandfather Gabriel's car and drove away.

Back in the house, Ginger helped Mom and Joshua with the dishes. Mom asked, "How did things go with Robin?"

Ginger shrugged. "All right, I guess."

Joshua said, "She sure didn't talk much at dinner."

"Maybe she felt strange her first time here," Mom said.

Ginger hoped that's all it was.

When they finished cleaning up, she headed for her room. Opening the door, she noticed that her white chenille spread was slightly rumpled where Robin must have snatched up her windbreaker. Oddly, it made Ginger feel upset.

She glanced at the bookshelf wall. Something was different . . . rearranged. The doll collection? There was the wooden shoe doll from Holland, the African doll, the Mexican doll— Where was the Japanese doll? The one in a kimona?

Her mind flashed to how oddly Robin had carried her windbreaker as she left. Had she hidden the doll under it? No one else could have been in the room . . . not even Lilabet or Joshua. But why would Robin do such an awful thing?

Lord, how can I love my neighbor, Ginger asked, *if my neighbor steals my stuff?*

The only answer that came back to her was: *Love your neighbor as yourself.*

5

The next day at school, Robin acted as if nothing had changed between them. Acting is what it was, Ginger thought resentfully. Then she remembered: *Love your neighbor as yourself.*

During Bible study, Miss Nordstrom read the other great commandment: "Love the Lord your God with all your heart and with all your soul and with all your mind."

"Do you really love God?" she asked.

Ginger stared at her freckled hands. She didn't know. God seemed wonderful to her, but was that loving Him?

Miss Nordstrom said, "We show our love for God by talking to Him . . . and by reading what He says to us in the Bible . . . and by doing what He asks us to do." She paused. "Let's discuss talking to Him. What's another word for that?"

Katie volunteered, "Praying."

"Yes, talking to Him is praying," Miss Nordstrom said. "That's fairly easy, but next comes reading the Bible."

Ginger said, "It's hard to read the Bible sometimes."

Miss Nordstrom said, "Perhaps you need to ask God to make you *want* to read it, then to help you understand what it says."

That's what I really want, Lord, Ginger thought—even though Robin was giving her a do-you-believe-this-stuff? look.

Miss Nordstrom said, "If we love God with all our heart and soul and mind, He helps us love our neighbor as ourselves."

Next, Miss Nordstrom began to discuss responsibilities—a reminder of having to work for Aunt Alice on Wednesday afternoons—soccer game day! Maybe Miss Nordstrom could help.

At recess, Ginger told her problem to her teacher.

"What a shame, Ginger," Miss Nordstrom said. "You're such a good soccer player. Can you work for her another day?"

"No. The nurse leaves at three o'clock, and Katie's mother takes Katie to piano lessons on Wednesday afternoons."

"Well, it's not as though they're scheduled league

56

games. Problems like this are why pickup games are best for middle grades," Miss Nordstrom said. "But it appears there's no way out of your dilemma unless God has other plans."

Despite Ginger's prayers, it seemed that God had no other plans. At school on Wednesday, the kids wailed, "But you and Cassie are our best soccer players!"

"I'm really sorry," Ginger apologized.

Katie said, "I didn't remember it was your soccer day."

After school Ginger's mother suggested, "Perhaps you can ask Aunt Alice about finding a replacement, but you did agree."

"Yeah." She'd agreed and it was almost three o'clock. She grabbed a handful of cheese crackers and said, "I'd better get going. Come on, Raffles."

As they reached the Camerons' brick patio, Ginger hoped Aunt Alice would find someone else to work for her next week—and not be too sick today.

Aunt Alice saw her through the screen. "I'm so glad to see you, Ginger. I've been looking forward to our visit all week. I'm glad you've brought Raffles again, too."

"Hello." A *Hi* seemed improper for such an elderly lady. On seeing her radiant smile, though, Ginger wondered. Aunt Alice seemed like a young girl trapped in an old body. Today her colorfully flowered bed jacket made her look even more joyous.

"You're just in time," she said. "Katie and her

mother had to leave a few minutes early, but I told them you'd be here exactly at three. I knew from our first meeting that you'd be reliable."

Uffff, Ginger thought, but she managed a polite, "Thank you."

"Won't you sit down?" Aunt Alice suggested.

As Ginger settled down on the chair by the bed, Aunt Alice said, "Katie told me about your wonderful birthday party and your elephant ride. How I'd love to have seen that!"

"It was fun all right," Ginger said. "I'd like to be a *mahout.* You know, the one who's in charge of the elephant."

"Would you now?" Aunt Alice asked. "I recall wishing the same thing years ago in India when I rode an elephant."

"You did? In India?"

"I surely did . . . wished to be a *mahout* and rode an elephant. But my ride must have been quite ordinary compared to your riding onstage to a cheering crowd. What a triumph!"

How differently Aunt Alice saw it than Robin! "It was wonderful," Ginger said. "I never dreamed I'd ride an elephant."

"Who knows what other wonders your life might hold?" Aunt Alice added, "If only I could see the Wild Animal Park myself."

"Mom and Grant bought a nice picture book about it. Maybe I could bring it next week." The moment Ginger said *next week,* she knew Aunt

58

Alice would expect her, and it seemed too late to do anything about it. She'd trapped herself.

"I'll surely look forward to that," Aunt Alice answered. "I've always been fond of animals."

Raffles had settled on the floor beside Ginger's chair, and he grinned as though he understood.

"How's your guardian angel duty?" Aunt Alice asked.

"Not so good." She told all about her problems with Robin, including the doll's disappearance.

"You're sure she took the doll?" Aunt Alice asked.

"I thought and thought about it, and no one else had a chance. I even asked Lilabet, and I can tell when she's fibbing."

"Did you tell your mother?"

Ginger shook her head. "She's so busy, I didn't want to. Besides, I want to do what we learned in Sunday school—love your neighbor as yourself."

"That's very commendable," Aunt Alice said. She raised her gray brows thoughtfully. "I wonder what the Lord would do. He tells us if someone smites us on one cheek, we are to turn the other to that person." She thought for a moment. "You say it's a collection doll that's missing?"

Ginger nodded.

"I wonder if you'd help me with something?" Aunt Alice asked. "I'd like to order another collection doll for Robin—let's say an India doll, since we've been talking about it—and next week, I'd like for you to give it to her."

59

"Give it? You mean really give it to her?!"

Aunt Alice said, "That's what I think the Lord would have us do. Please hand me the telephone book."

Ginger gave it to her.

Before long, Aunt Alice had called Santa Rosita Toys, asked them to deliver an India doll to the house, gift-wrapped, and charged it to her account. She turned to Ginger. "Promise you'll pray as often as you can for Robin, and I will, too. And let's keep this our secret, all right?"

"All right," Ginger answered uneasily.

Aunt Alice lay back against her pillow, smiling. "Now that we've taken care of that bit of business, I'd love to hear the psalms. Here's my Bible. Why don't we begin with my favorite, Psalm 100? It should be by the marking ribbon."

Ginger opened the Bible to the maroon ribbon and found Psalm 100. She read aloud:

"Shout for joy to the Lord, all the earth.
Worship the Lord with gladness;
come before him with joyful songs.
Know that the Lord is God.
It is he who made us, and we are his;
we are his people, the sheep of his pasture.
Enter his gates with thanksgiving
and his courts with praise;
give thanks to him and praise his name.
For the Lord is good and his love endures
forever;

his faithfulness continues through all
generations."

"Why do you look so surprised?" Aunt Alice
asked.

Ginger said, "This morning at Bible study I told
Miss Nordstrom that sometimes it's hard to understand the Bible. She said maybe I should ask God to
make me want to read it and ask him to help me
understand what it says, so I did."

"And?"

Ginger smiled. "Being here with you, I wanted to
read it. And I truly understood what it said."

Aunt Alice laughed. "The Lord answered your
prayer. He always does. He has three answers to
prayer . . . yes, no, or later. *If* we ask, He always
answers."

"I'm going to really start praying for Robin,"
Ginger announced with determination.

"Why don't we begin right now?" Aunt Alice suggested and held out her hand to pray.

On Thursday and Friday, however, Robin wasn't
in school.

On Saturday, Aunt Alice phoned Ginger. "Our
'turn the other cheek' doll has been delivered. Can
you take it to Robin?"

The idea seemed crazy now, but Ginger said,
"Sure. I'm coming."

"You might want to ride your bicycle," Aunt
Alice suggested. "I understand that the Lindbergs
live nearly a mile away."

When Ginger arrived at the Camerons' house on her bike, Aunt Alice seemed as excited as ever about their project. "I can't wait to hear how it's received. Please phone me."

Ginger asked nervously, "What shall I say to Robin?"

"The Lord will help you know what to say," Aunt Alice promised. "These kinds of things always seem to turn out differently from what one expects. You go now, and I'll pray."

Taking the silver and white package, Ginger rode off on her bike. She grew more and more nervous as she approached Robin's house. Praying, she pedaled to the back door where they picked up Robin for school every morning.

Ginger climbed off her bike, fluffed up the package's white ribbon, and headed for the door. She knocked, chewing her gum hard. The house was silent.

She knocked again.

Silence.

Relieved, Ginger set the package by the door, jumped on her bike, and sped wildly away.

"Good morning, Robin," Grant said when they picked her up for school the next Monday morning. "I hope you're feeling better." As usual, he'd climbed out of the car to open the back door for her.

"Thanks," she answered bleakly. She climbed in and sat down beside Ginger without a glance. If

Robin had received the India doll, she didn't act like it. She looked as glum as ever in her familiar blackish-blue dress.

Ginger's eyes darted to Mrs. Lindberg's back door, where she'd left the present, but there was no sign of it.

Katie sat on the other side of Ginger, and she leaned forward to ask Robin, "Did you have a good weekend?"

"It was all right," Robin answered, though her tone clearly meant it had been dull, dull, dull.

Ginger told her, "I should have phoned, but I knew you were sick. Anyhow, I usually go to my Grandmother Trumbell's house at the beach on Saturdays. This week, though, my dad was out of town, so she came home after church with us."

She babbled on, even though it was no one's business that she hadn't seen Dad this weekend or plenty of others. He sold surfboards to shops all over the West Coast—and it hurt to know selling them seemed more important to him than seeing her. Anyhow, Robin Lindberg wasn't the only one with problems.

As they drove on, the car was so quiet that Ginger finally asked Robin, "Did you do any acting this weekend?"

Robin shot her a mind-your-own-business glance.

Ginger clamped her mouth shut and rearranged her blue denim book bag on the lap of her green skirt. At least she'd tried to be friendly.

Instead of arriving at school early as usual, they rushed to the playground just in time to hear the morning buzzer. Ginger headed for the flagpoles with Robin and Katie, and they joined Miss Nordstrom and their fifth-grade classmates.

Mr. Adams, the elementary principal, led the pledges of allegiance. Ginger knew the Christian pledge now, too, and spoke it firmly, "I pledge allegiance to the Christian flag and to the Savior for whose kingdom it stands. One Savior, crucified, risen, and coming again." Maybe she didn't know a lot about being a Christian yet, but she was learning. The hardest part by far, it seemed, was loving your neighbor as yourself.

Mr. Adams said, "We'll be having Bible Character Day on October 31 again this year. You can dress like any biblical person, except the Lord. And no devils or witches or other evil spirits."

An angel . . . that's what she wanted to be! Ginger thought. She'd copy the carved wooden angel Grandfather had given her for her birthday.

Mr. Adams continued, "Last year we had Moses, Mary, Joseph, Queen Esther, and Ruth, and we also had lots of Romans, Greeks, and Egyptians. In the morning, each class will parade through the other classrooms. . . ."

Everyone was excited as they hurried to their classrooms. Ginger asked Robin, "Who are you going to be?"

"Maybe I'll be sick again," Robin answered.

So Robin had only pretended to be sick last Thursday and Friday. Ginger wasn't surprised. Suddenly inspiration hit. "It'll be a wonderful chance for acting and costumes, Robin. Are you good at making costumes?"

"Sure I am," Robin retorted. "I can make scenery, too."

"Did you learn that from library books?" Ginger asked.

Robin replied grouchily, "Leave me alone!"

"If that's what you want. I'm really sorry if I hurt your feelings."

Robin shot her a nasty look, and Ginger guessed all she could do now for Robin was pray. She was already on the whole family's prayer list and Aunt Alice's, too, but so far it hadn't done any good.

When all the kids were settled at their desks, Miss Nordstrom said, "Good morning! I thought it'd be interesting if our class had a special Bible Character Day discussion, too. We will tell about our characters and about the time in which they lived, as well as their relationships to God."

Robin whispered to Ginger, "What are you going to be?"

"An angel," she answered.

"That's what I'd planned myself," Robin said.

I'll bet, Ginger thought.

Robin whispered, "How are you going to make the wings?"

"I don't know yet. I've got a book about angels."

Mom could make a white robe, she figured, and Dad could make the frame for the angel wings. If he wasn't still mad at her for going to a Christian school. . . .

Up front by the blackboard, Miss Nordstrom said, "I'd like you to work on your word warm-up first."

Ginger, still thinking about her angel costume, got out her workbook. She'd leave a message with Gram saying, "I really have to see him." Feeling a little crazy, she whispered to Robin, "My dad can help both of us with our angel wings Saturday, and Gram can sew them. She's a seamstress. You can come to her house with me."

"Girls!" Miss Nordstrom warned them.

Ginger opened her notebook, not waiting for Robin's reply. She probably wouldn't want to do it. Besides, now that she thought about it, the idea of taking Robin to Gram's on Saturday seemed dumb, dumb, dumb. For one thing, she might steal something. For another, who knew if Dad would even come? She hoped she hadn't gotten herself into another mess.

6

By Wednesday Ginger was resigned to missing another soccer game. After school, she and Joshua returned home and found Mom at work in the family room on their Bible character costumes, her sewing machine humming. Joshua inspected his brown burlap Moses robe.

"Guess I'd better start making my white hair and beard," he said.

"Why don't you grow 'em?" Ginger teased as she grabbed an apple from the fruit bowl on the table.

"Why don't you grow angel wings?" he returned. Grinning, he left to try on the robe.

Mom sewed up a long seam on the white angel robe. "Any thoughts on making the wings?"

Ginger munched on her apple. "I—I was thinking Dad might like to help. He's good at stuff like that."

"Yes, he is," her mother agreed.

For an instant, Ginger feared Mom might question his reliability, but she didn't. Instead, she said, "The robe should be finished when you come home from Aunt Alice's. You can try it on then."

"Okay. Can I, I mean *may* I take the Wild Animal Park book to show her?" Ginger asked. "Aunt Alice would like to see it."

"What a good idea!" Her mother lined up the white material for another seam. "You might like to take your birthday outing pictures, too. They're on the hall chest."

"Yeah, she'd probably like to see them," Ginger decided. She finished her apple and hook shot the core into the wastebasket. "See you later. Come on, Raffles, we're visiting Aunt Alice." Ginger hadn't talked with her since Saturday, when she'd phoned about leaving the doll at Lindbergs' back door.

Upon their arrival, they found the elderly lady propped against her bed pillows, her blue eyes sparkling. "I can't wait to hear what Robin said about the doll appearing on her doorstep."

"She didn't say a thing about it, not one thing," Ginger answered. "I looked by her back door Monday morning when we picked her up. The package wasn't there anymore."

"If only we could have watched her opening it,"

68

Aunt Alice said. "What a rare moment that must have been."

"I guess so," Ginger replied. "Anyway, I brought the pictures from my birthday outing, so you can see what Robin looks like. I brought the Wild Animal Park book, too."

"Wonderful." Aunt Alice reached for her reading glasses on the nightstand. "At last, I'm going to get a look at Katie's and your classmates. Why don't you bring the chair closer to my bed so you can tell me who everyone is."

Ginger pulled the chair next to the bed and began to look at the pictures with her. After a while she said, "Here's Robin when we posed on the rhino. She's the one trying to look important."

"Hmmm . . . so she is. She'd probably be pretty if she'd stop hiding behind her hair."

"That's what I think, too," Ginger said. "And here she is, grouchy while everyone was singing happy birthday to me."

"She does look unhappy," Aunt Alice answered. She examined the other pictures. "Yes, I'd say Robin is thoroughly miserable. I hope the doll we sent didn't shock her too much."

"I doubt that!" Ginger said.

"It must be difficult for her to cope with life."

Aunt Alice was compassionate like Katie, Ginger decided. Probably she should be more compassionate herself. "Let me tell you the other girls' names," she offered.

Aunt Alice looked through all of the pictures twice. "My very favorite is this one of you riding the elephant and waving as if you're the Queen of Sheba," she said. "It deserves a distinguished title. Let me think . . . yes, I have it . . . 'Ginger Trumbell, World-Famous Mahout.' "

Ginger laughed.

"I'd love to have a copy of it," Aunt Alice said.

"I'll bet Mom would get one for you," Ginger replied. "I'll ask her to make a copy of this one on the rhino, too. Katie looks just right. Kind and friendly like usual."

After they'd looked through the pictures in the Wild Animal Park book, Aunt Alice said, "Your family is spoiling me. This morning your grandfather brought over the picture of the guardian angel you'd told me about. Not only was it wonderful, but you'd described it perfectly. It's a special talent to be able to describe something so well that the other person can see it in their mind's eye, too. Perhaps you should be a writer."

"You think so?" Ginger asked, trying not to look pleased.

"I think you should pray for God's leading about it," Aunt Alice said. She removed her glasses. "What's new at school?"

"We're going to have Bible Character Day instead of Halloween. We just found out Monday."

"Katie mentioned it, too," Aunt Alice said. "What are you going to be?" She was so interested that

70

Ginger even told about Robin copying the idea of being an angel.

Aunt Alice said, "It's an excellent idea for your father to help make the angel wings—and a fine idea to include Robin." Suddenly her eyes widened and she clutched her stomach in pain. "Please hand me those pills . . . and a glass of water."

"Sure—" Ginger replied, hurrying to help.

Aunt Alice took a pill, then lay back against her pillow. "Thank you, Ginger." She closed her eyes and seemed to be praying. A long time later, she drifted off to sleep, while Ginger sat on the edge of her chair and watched nervously.

Saturday afternoon Mom drove Ginger and Robin to Gram's house by the beach. Mom glanced at Ginger in the rearview mirror. "Are you certain your father will be there?"

"Gram told me she'd say it was really important," Ginger replied. She chewed her gum harder and harder. Bible Character Day was this Monday . . . *this* Monday! As if that weren't bad enough, she was bringing a girl to Gram's house who lied and stole. She'd have to keep an eye on her.

She glanced at Robin, who was twisting her long hair around to the front of her neck as usual. She'd worn faded jeans and the dark blue blouse again, while Ginger was dressed in a bright yellow shorts outfit.

It was already after one o'clock when they pulled

up in front of Gram's old white house. There was no sign of Dad's sports car. Gram rose from the front porch swing and waved at them as Ginger and Robin climbed out of the car.

"I guess your father's late," Mom said. "Maybe he's out buying wire for the wings."

"Yeah," Ginger said, doubting it. She hadn't said anything to Gram about needing wire, but of course Mom might have mentioned it when she phoned Gram about what time they'd come.

Gram started down the sidewalk, smiling broadly. "How's my favorite angel?" she asked. She looked perky, and her short salt-and-pepper curls shone in the afternoon sunlight.

Ginger laughed, and Gram gave her a good hug. "This is Robin Lindberg, Gram."

"Always pleased to meet a friend of Ginger's, especially another angel," Gram said. She reached a hand out to Robin.

"Hi," Robin said, keeping her hands to herself.

Gram smiled anyhow. "You have the most beautiful dark blue eyes. You're not wearing those colored contact lenses, are you?"

"No, I'm not!" Robin answered in a huff.

"I didn't mean to insult you," Gram said. "I'd like to be friends. In fact, I've got a piece of bright blue cotton that would really do justice to your eyes."

Robin gave her a suspicious look.

"Gram makes suits, coats, and dresses—all kinds of clothes for people," Ginger explained. "Mom says

72

she's the best seamstress in Santa Rosita."

"None of that flattery," Gram objected. "Besides, there are only two seamstresses in town!" Grinning, she stuck her head into Mom's car to ask about being picked up for church tomorrow.

Before driving away, Mom called back to them, "I'll be back at four o'clock. Have fun, and get those wings done!"

Ginger said to Gram, "It's not going to give us much time for making the wings. When's Dad coming?"

Gram shrugged unhappily. "He wasn't sure." She brightened. "Come on in," she said. "I can't wait to show you the fabric I have for your wings."

In the house, Gram had already spread the gold-threaded white fabric across the living room couch. "What do you think?"

"It's perfect," Ginger replied.

Even Robin was impressed with the fabric, though not with Gram's modest house or old furniture.

Gram told them, "I bought the cloth years ago for almost nothing at a sale. I'm glad it won't be rotting in my closet." She turned to Robin. "There's plenty for your wings, too."

"Thanks," Robin said in a lukewarm tone.

Gram told Ginger, "While we wait for your father, I'm going to find that blue fabric that was made for Robin's eyes. Why don't you two go out back and play ping-pong?"

"You want to play ping-pong?" Ginger asked.

"I don't like sports," Robin reminded her testily.

Ginger gave her gum a loud snap. "Well, let's go sit on the porch swing and wait for Dad." If nothing else, Robin might not be tempted to steal anything there.

Outside on the swing, Ginger said, "I wish we could go walk on the beach, but I guess we'd better wait here. Did you get your angel robe sewn?"

"I'm finishing it. Our sewing machine's broken."

Ginger asked, "You mean you sewed it all by hand?"

"What else?" Robin complained.

They sat swinging, not saying much, until Gram came out with the sky blue material and held it up to Robin. "Exactly right," she pronounced. "How'd you like me to make you a casual top like Ginger has on right now?"

Robin's eyes turned hopeful, but only for an instant. "No-thanks."

"I should have explained it'd be a present," Gram said. "You're about the same size as Ginger, and I have an easy pattern. It'd be done in less than an hour."

Ginger saw that Robin really wanted to say yes, but she repeated, "No-thanks."

"Well," Gram said, sitting down on one of her white wicker rocking chairs. "Tell me about school, girls."

They talked for a long time, until Gram's clock

74

bonged out two o'clock. Gram suggested, "Why don't you girls go walking on the beach? I'll send your father down for you when he comes."

Ginger's spirits sank, but she said, "We won't wander off too far, so he can find us."

Fifteen minutes later, she and Robin walked barefooted in the sand alongside the surf. Great waves gathered in the distance and roared in on the beach; they crashed across the sand and left a rim of foam at their feet.

Robin still didn't talk, but the roar of the ocean filled the quietness. It was the kind of a place where problems didn't seem quite so bad, Ginger thought. It had been the place where she'd turned to God. After a while she told Robin, "This is my favorite place in the whole world."

Robin looked out at the nearby cliffs without answering.

"What was it like in New Orleans?" Ginger asked.

Robin shrugged. "We had the Mississippi River and big ships sailing by."

"That must have been something!" Ginger replied.

"It always looked like there were wonderful places to go and see," Robin said. "You know, to go traveling."

"Did you travel a lot?"

"When I was little, but I don't remember. Mostly I remember living in New Orleans." Robin's voice took on a tone of great importance. "We lived in a southern mansion, then my family died in a fire. The whole mansion burned down."

Another lie, Ginger thought, but out loud she said, "I'm sorry. It must have been nice, though, living in a mansion."

"It was wonderful," Robin said, making it sound true. "And it was wonderful to live in New Orleans. Millions of tourists come . . . and there was a big world fair near our apartment—" She stopped, turned red, and explained too quickly, "We had an apartment in town, besides the mansion."

"Oh, yeah?" Ginger asked, not convinced. She glanced down at her watch. Almost three o'clock. After a while she said, "You don't talk southern like Katie."

Robin lifted her chin. "I didn't always live there."

At three-thirty, Ginger said, "We'd better start back for Gram's house. I guess Dad was too busy to make it. Only now I don't know how we'll get our wings made in time."

Robin darted an I-figured glance at her.

At the house, Gram looked upset and her voice sounded stiff. "After you left, your dad phoned to say he couldn't get here. I thought you might as well enjoy the beach."

Ginger felt numb, then her lower lip began to tremble. She turned away and prayed, *Lord, don't let me cry here in front of them. And don't let me be mad at him again, either.*

Gram said, "Robin, that blue fabric had your name written all over it, so I made you a top after all."

"You did?" Robin asked with disbelief.

"I did." Gram thrust the shirt at her. "Just go down the hall to my bedroom and try it on. Nothing leaves this house if it doesn't fit right. I've got my reputation to consider."

Robin looked at her uncertainly. "Okay." She took the blue top and started for the bedroom, then turned to say a shaky, "Thanks, Mrs. Trumbell."

"Not at all," Gram answered with a wink at Ginger.

When the bedroom door closed behind Robin, Ginger said, "That was really nice of you, Gram."

"I couldn't let the whole afternoon be a loss," Gram said. "At least she'll know we care."

"It's not easy to be friends with some people."

"No, it isn't," Gram agreed, "sometimes even when they're in your own family."

Gram gazed at her, and Ginger understood.

"We can't let your father get us down, Ginger. He might be far from perfect, but he loves each of us as much as he can."

"I guess he probably does." Ginger let out a discouraged breath. "Only sometimes, Gram, it seems like he *wants* me to give up on him. But you know what? I'm never ever in all of my life going to. How about you?"

Gram looked equally determined. "Then we'll

77

never give up on him together!"

"And I'm not giving up on Robin, either," Ginger decided. "I keep trying to remember, 'love your neighbor as yourself.' "

"I'm glad to hear it," Gram said, giving Ginger a hug.

7

Mom picked them up at exactly four o'clock. "I bought wire for the angel wing frames," she said.

Ginger bristled. "How'd you know Dad didn't come?"

"I phoned Gram. We decided there wasn't any time to lose and that I'd better buy the wire."

"Oh." Ginger decided not to say more about Dad not coming, no matter how badly it hurt to be let down again. "Thanks, Mom," she added.

She glanced at Robin, who was giving her another I-figured look. *Well!* Ginger thought. At least her own father wasn't in jail like Robin's for selling drugs.

As they drove home, Mom said, "Gram's coming

over tomorrow after church to help sew the wings. Robin, if you'll stay tonight for pizza, we should have time to make the wing frames for you, too. That is, if you want help."

"I don't have much choice," Robin grumbled. "I'll have to call home."

"Of course," Mom replied. "You can phone your great-grandmother from our house. If it's not all right with her, I'll drive you on home."

"Okay," Robin replied, twisting her hair in front of her neck. She wore the new sky blue top with her jeans, and the color did brighten her up. She had told Gram, "I get sick of wearing my cousin's old school uniforms." That explained why she always wore blackish-blue.

When they arrived at home, Ginger showed Robin to the family room phone. Then she set the table, half keeping an eye on Robin. A good thing that not much in the house, except big pieces of antique furniture, was worth stealing.

When Robin hung up the phone, she said to Ginger's mother, "I can stay, but not too late."

"Wonderful," Mom replied as she tore up lettuce for the salad. She glanced up as the door opened. "Here's Grandfather . . . just in time, too."

"In time for what?" he asked with a suspicious grin.

"The girls want to be angels for Bible Character Day at school Monday," Mom said. "Can you make angel wing frames?"

"That's one thing I can do," he replied. "We've had many an angel in church Christmas plays. Let's go out to the garage. It sounds like time is of the essence."

"It sure is," Ginger said. "Come on, Robin."

Robin came along, eyeing Grandfather Gabriel nervously.

Just like the first time she'd met him herself, Ginger remembered. She'd thought ministers were sort of spooky, as if they knew special things about God—and maybe about people, too.

Grandfather said, "Let's see what we can do to turn you two into reasonable looking angels . . . if that's possible!"

Even Robin smiled at that.

In the garage, he sketched angel wings on paper, then cut the wire to size. He didn't act perfect or holy for Robin, but then he never did. Before long, he'd fashioned the wire into angel wings—and jollied Ginger and Robin into good moods. "Now it's up to our seamstress to make the wings look good," he said, "and if I know Gram, she will."

Grant drove up with Joshua and Lilabet, who got out of the car carrying hot pizzas. Grant said, "We've got the makings for hot fudge sundaes, too. Who's hungry?"

"Who isn't?" Grandfather chuckled. "Just in time. We've finished our angel wing frames. Lead on!"

"Come on," Ginger said, leading Robin to the

house. At least she didn't look as distrustful of them as the first time she'd visited. Not that Robin was so trustworthy herself!

Sunday night Gram finished the angel wings, and Mrs. Lindberg brought Robin over so she could try on hers, too. Glancing at her angel wings in the mirror, Ginger said, "They really do look wonderful."

"I could have made them myself," Robin said.

So why didn't you? Ginger felt like asking.

"What are you going to tell about angels in our class talk?" Robin inquired.

"I wrote a report," Ginger said, nodding at the neat copy of her talk on the desk. "Come on."

Halfway down the hall, she turned and was surprised to see Robin just coming out of the door. "What's wrong?"

"I'm having trouble getting used to the wings," Robin said.

On Monday morning, they put the angel wings into the trunk of Grant's car, but they wore their white robes and golden halos.

Katie was dressed as a raggedy servant. "The Lord told us to be like servants to others," she explained.

Joshua wore white cotton hair and a beard and his brown burlap Moses robe, and he carried a thick stick.

As they drove along the freeway, people in other cars stared and pointed at them. Grant was the only one in regular clothes because the high school wasn't having Bible Character Day. "I should have dressed as a Roman soldier and hired a chariot to drive on the freeway," he laughed. "Then they'd really have had something to wake them up this morning!"

At school, everyone wore biblical costumes, even Mr. Adams, who was dressed like Joseph in a coat of many colors. Miss Nordstrom was Ruth and wore a blue robe. Ginger almost laughed at the little boys dressed like old prophets; their beards were so long, they looked like they'd trip over them. Others were soldiers wearing aluminum foil suits of armor. They all made a strange sight saying the morning pledges of allegiance by the flagpoles, then going to their classrooms.

In class, Ginger noticed that Robin's white robe was not as neatly made as her own. Not that it mattered, but maybe Robin couldn't make things as well as she'd claimed. As they sat down at their desks, she remarked to Robin, "Looks like we have to hang our wings over the backs of our chairs."

Robin retorted, "Don't you think I know that?"

Ginger flinched. Why was Robin so snappy and nervous?

Miss Nordstrom stood up front and said her usual, "Good morning to you, class." She smiled. "Doesn't it look as if we've stepped back into history! Why don't each of you tell a little about your biblical character before the class parade?"

Ginger listened as, one by one, kids stood up front to tell who they were. Some read from notes. Between talks, she glanced at her own notes. *My Bible character is an angel. Angels are spiritual messengers from God. Angels are mentioned nearly three hundred times in the Bible. . . .* She'd memorized that, but she'd have to read the rest of it. It was awful to wait in the last row, and she grew more nervous as her turn approached. Robin would be first.

Finally Miss Nordstrom said, "Robin Lindberg."

Robin stood up carefully so her wings wouldn't catch on her chair. She walked up the aisle, showing off the beautiful gold-threaded wings. Turning, she smiled proudly and began to speak without notes. "My Bible character is an angel. Angels are spiritual messengers from God. Angels are mentioned nearly three hundred times in the Bible. . . ."

Her own words! How did Robin get them? Ginger's mind flew to last night in her bedroom when they'd tried on the angel wings. The talk had been on her desk and messy copies of it in the wastebasket. Robin must have stolen one!

While Robin spoke on, Ginger recalled Robin taking Mom's chance to volunteer at the bird show, then trying to volunteer at the elephant show. That's exactly what she was doing here: stealing the show!

When Robin finished, she bobbed a little curtsy, returned to her seat, and sat down carefully so her wings wouldn't catch on the chair.

Miss Nordstrom said, "That was very good, Robin. Where did you and Ginger get the idea to be angels?"

Robin answered, "It was *my* idea."

Uffffffffffffff, Ginger thought.

"It certainly was a good idea," Miss Nordstrom said with a pleased smile at Robin. "Now, Ginger, would you tell us something more about angels?"

Trying to hide her anger, Ginger stood up without thinking. Right away, her angel wings caught on the back of the chair. The kids laughed while she struggled to get them loose. At last she had her robe and wings straight, and went forward. She looked at Miss Nordstrom and her classmates. What could she say? The school rules said you shouldn't tattle. What could she do without being meaner than ever to Robin?

She cleared her throat and began. "My Bible character is an angel. Like Robin said, angels are spiritual messengers from God. And, like she said, angels are mentioned—" Embarrassed and madder by the instant, Ginger stopped. "Well, Robin told all of it."

Everyone laughed a little, and Ginger tore off for her seat, not looking at anyone. She sat down, catching her wings on top of her chair, then had to stand and twist around to adjust them. She hadn't felt so unangelic since she'd become a Christian. How she'd like to beat up Robin Lindberg so badly she'd never steal or lie or cheat again!

As soon as everyone turned away, she hissed at Robin, "Why did you do that?"

Robin raised her chin and glared at her. "Do what?"

"You know what!" Ginger snapped.

Miss Nordstrom warned, "Angels, please—"

Ginger grabbed a deep breath and prayed, *Help me with my temper, Lord! And please help me with Robin Lindberg!*

8

At dinner Grandfather asked, "How did Bible Character Day go?"

"It's more for little kids," Joshua said, "but it was fun anyhow."

"How about you, Ginger?" Grant asked.

She swallowed a mouthful of tuna casserole, the hurt of the morning flooding through her again. Walking behind Robin in the parade from class to class, it had been hard to smile and look angelic. "It wasn't a good day," she said. To her dismay, tears welled up in her eyes.

"Why, Ginger," Mom said, "whatever went wrong?"

"Robin stole my idea to be an angel," Ginger

blurted, "and then she stole my talk for class!"

Grant's fork stopped halfway to his mouth. "Are you sure?"

Ginger nodded. "And that's not all she stole! She stole the Japanese doll from my collection! And I'll bet she stole the dollar from Mom's blouse sleeve at the Wild Animal Park so she could be in the bird show!"

"I wondered where that dollar disappeared to," Mom said. "The amphitheater stands were solid, so it couldn't have fallen through. I'm sorry to admit that I suspected Robin myself, especially when she stood up waving the dollar bill."

"Those are serious accusations," Grant said. "Ginger, perhaps you'd better tell us more about them. Let's start with your Japanese doll."

She hesitated, then made herself tell. "The first time Robin was here, when you invited Mrs. Lindberg for dinner, too, Robin said she liked the collection dolls because of their costumes. You know, she likes acting and costumes and stuff. Just before you drove them home, Robin went to my bathroom. I saw her from the hallway, and she yelled she could find her own way. Anyhow, when she came out, she was carrying her windbreaker all stiff and funny like there was something in it. And when I went back to my room, my doll was gone."

"It does sound suspicious," Grant said, "but it doesn't prove anything. What's this about her stealing your talk?"

"When we tried on the angel costumes in my bedroom, she asked what I'd say in class, and I told her I'd written a talk. I think she took a copy from my wastebasket."

"Why do you think so?" Mom asked.

"Because in class she used my exact words!" Ginger replied. "Besides, when I came down the hallway to show you the costume Sunday night, she took too long following me. She pretended her wings had gotten stuck."

"It's difficult to believe anyone could do that," Mom said, "especially since the costumes were for *angels!*"

Grandfather replied, "When people are entirely self-centered, it's amazing what they will do."

"I think she lies, too," Ginger added. "At the Wild Animal Park she wanted to be the elephant show volunteer, and she told me it was her birthday. And the other day at the beach, she talked about her family's mansion in New Orleans, then she goofed and said 'apartment.' Of course, *then* she said they'd had an apartment, too."

"Hmmmmm," Grandfather began. "Mrs. Lindberg has confided in me, and I try not to reveal confidences, but I will say that Ginger is probably right. Robin has a lot of problems."

Lilabet had listened to every word, and she said with indignation, "Rob-in is bad!"

Grandfather said to her, "Maybe way deep in her heart, Lilabet, Robin wants to be good. Maybe she just doesn't know *how* to be good yet."

Mom asked, "Why didn't you tell us sooner, Ginger? This can't have been easy for you."

Ginger shrugged. "You were all so busy. Besides, I told Aunt Alice. She bought another collection doll for Robin and had me deliver it to her door. Like turning the other cheek."

Grandfather raised his gray brows. "A good idea."

"We'll have to redouble our prayers for Robin," Grant said. "And our prayers for you, Ginger."

Wednesday afternoon, Ginger hadn't planned to tell Aunt Alice all about it. But when the elderly lady awakened from her nap and began to ask questions, Ginger gave in.

After listening carefully, Aunt Alice said, "I'm sorry to hear it, especially for your sake. What's happened with her since Monday . . . since Bible Character Day?"

"Not much," Ginger answered. "She acts like nothing is different between us. Like she didn't do a single thing wrong."

Aunt Alice said, "We're to give thanks in all things, Ginger, even when we don't understand. So let's give thanks in this, too." She held her hand out for Ginger to pray.

"Thank You, Lord, for bringing Robin into our lives," Aunt Alice began. "We thank You in spite of all of the trouble she's caused, because we know You can turn troubles into wonders. We ask that You would guide our dear Ginger and give her Your love for Robin. . . ."

At school the next morning Miss Nordstrom announced, "I'd like each of you to start thinking about a play for Thanksgiving. It's only two and a half weeks away."

Ginger watched Robin brighten with excitement.

As it turned out, Ginger had plenty of time to plan a play. Friday and the next week she was home with a strep throat. Katie caught it, too, so she didn't go to piano lessons on Wednesday, and Ginger didn't have to work for Aunt Alice.

When Ginger returned to class the next Monday, she couldn't believe what had happened. Miss Nordstrom said, "Time to practice our plays," and everyone gathered into groups. The girls in the class gathered around Robin Lindberg, who'd written a Thanksgiving play for all of them—except her. By the time Ginger realized it and looked for Miss Nordstrom to see if she'd noticed, the teacher was just stepping out of the room.

Ginger said to Katie, "I thought we were supposed to write individual plays—you know, soliloquies. Mom brought me a library book about pilgrims, so I wrote about a pilgrim girl."

"Robin wrote a good play," Katie said, "but I was absent most of the time, and I surely thought you'd be in it, too."

"Well, I'm not! How can all of the girls in the class be in a play except me? How could it happen?"

Katie said, "I don't know, but you know how Robin is. Do you want me to do something to help?"

"No, thanks," Ginger said. "I'll take care of it myself."

She headed over to Robin's group. When she was able to speak privately to Robin, Ginger made herself ask, "Can I be in your play, too, Robin?"

"There's no room for more characters," Robin retorted.

"You mean there's no room for me?" Ginger asked.

Robin's dark blue eyes glittered. "No room."

Ginger turned away. Feeling wretched, she returned to her desk to stare at her soliloquy. The more she stared at it, the more awful it seemed. It was unfair about Robin's play, especially since her family had been so nice to Robin. This very day she was wearing the top Gram had made for her! Ginger glanced over at the girls practicing together and wished that they weren't having so much fun.

After play practice, Miss Nordstrom said, "For art today, we'll make pilgrim hats."

At least she wouldn't be left out of that, Ginger thought.

The boys made Indian headbands or tall black hats with white bands and buckles in front. The girls made white pilgrim lady hats that were stiff around the face and had puffy crepe paper crowns.

Usually she wasn't too good at art projects, but even Miss Nordstrom remarked, "My, Ginger, didn't your hat turn out well!"

Ginger noticed that Robin, in her impatience, had poked her finger through the crepe paper when she stretched it out for puffiness. The harder Robin tried, the worse it looked.

Miss Nordstrom said, "When you're finished, please use a pencil to write your name in your hat. We'll hang them by our windows so our room looks festive for Thanksgiving."

The doctor didn't want Ginger going outside to play yet, and she had plenty of makeup work to do in the classroom. One morning Miss Norstrom stopped at Ginger's desk while the other kids were outside for recess.

"Ginger," she said, "I've just realized that all of the other girls are in Robin's play. Shall I ask her to include you, too?"

"No, thanks," Ginger answered, not wanting to be forced upon Robin or anyone else.

"You're sure?" Miss Nordstrom asked.

Ginger nodded. "I'm sure. Thanks."

The week dragged by, and play practice made her feel worse every day. Pride, awful old pride. That's what made her turn down Katie's and Miss Nordstrom's offers to get her into Robin's play, Ginger thought.

Rain fell heavily Thanksgiving week, and lots of people got sick, including Miss Nordstrom.

On Wednesday after lunch Mrs. Mackie, the substitute, said, "Time for our Thanksgiving plays, class. Girls, please get your pilgrim lady hats first."

Ginger headed for the rain-spattered windows with the rest of the girls and began to take her hat down.

Robin said loudly, "That's my hat!"

"It's got my name in it," Ginger said, turning it over to show Robin. To her amazement, the inside of the hat said *Robin Lindberg*.

Robin grabbed it from her. "I told you, it's my hat."

Bewildered, Ginger looked for her hat, but all of the other white pilgrim lady hats were taken.

Mrs. Mackie asked, "What's the problem, girls?"

"I can't find my hat," Ginger explained.

Mrs. Mackie asked, "Are you sure they didn't make them when you were out sick?"

"I made one," Ginger assured her. "I really did."

Mrs. Mackie asked, "Will all of you girls check to be sure that your name is in your hat?"

Every girl had her own hat, and it didn't take Ginger long to guess what had happened. Robin had thrown out her own ruined hat and stolen Ginger's! But how could she prove it?

Mrs. Mackie said, "With such pretty red hair, Ginger, you don't need a hat."

Ha, Ginger thought. She wouldn't look like a pilgrim.

As if that weren't bad enough, Mrs. Mackie said,

"I see you're signed up for a soliloquy, Ginger. Why don't you go first?"

Heartsick, Ginger rose from her chair and started forward. Probably it'd been a mistake to write a serious play about how the pilgrims suffered, but it was too late now. She tried to remember Grandfather's advice: "Speak with emotion, with passion, as if it's all real to you." Standing before the class, she saw everyone wearing their pilgrim hats and Indian headbands, which made her feel worse.

"Go ahead, Ginger," Mrs. Mackie urged.

Ginger swallowed hard. "My name is Priscilla," she began. "I came to the New World on a ship named the *Mayflower*. . . ."

To her dismay, the kids began to laugh. Worst of all, their laughter had started in the back row with Robin.

"It's not supposed to be funny!" Ginger snapped.

Mrs. Mackie warned, "Class, let's be polite."

The kids settled down, but it was all ruined anyhow. Instead of speaking with emotion, Ginger's words fell as drearily as the rain outside the windows.

When it was over, the kids clapped politely, and Ginger pressed her lips together hard so they wouldn't tremble as she returned to her seat.

"Thank you, Ginger," Mrs. Mackie said. "That was very interesting."

Yeah, Ginger thought. *Interesting and terrible.*

Next, five boys did a silly play, then it was time

for Robin and the rest of the girls. Their play was about pilgrims and Indians almost having trouble until a girl named Prudence saved them by giving an Indian named Red Feather her bracelet. Prudence, of course, was played by none other than Robin Lindberg.

"Very good," Mrs. Mackie said as everyone applauded, but Ginger knew it was a lot better than just "very good." Robin's play was perfectly wonderful.

The afternoon dragged on, as depressing as the rain.

Later, as they drove home, Mrs. Cameron wasn't sure she wanted to take Katie to piano lessons. When they arrived in their neighborhood, it was already late because of the rain-flooded streets. Finally Mrs. Cameron decided they'd go to piano lessons anyway. Dropping Ginger off at their house, she said, "Be sure to call your mother and let her know you're here, Ginger."

"I will," Ginger promised and dashed out into the rain.

She let herself into the Camerons' house, her yellow slicker and hat dripping. She took them off in the entry and headed for Aunt Alice's room.

"Oh, you must be Ginger—" the nurse said, blocking her from the bedroom. "We won't be needing you today, dear. I've just had to call the doctor. I'll stay. You can go on home."

Ginger caught a glimpse of Aunt Alice in bed. She

looked awful, all shriveled up with pain. "Is she . . . is she going to be okay?"

The nurse said, "It's difficult to say."

Appalled, Ginger hurried back for her slicker and hat and, pulling them on, ran home through the rain. *God, please don't let Aunt Alice be in such pain!* she prayed. She didn't want her to die, but she didn't want her to hurt so badly either.

When she opened the family room door, the smell of pumpkin pies comforted her a little. Mom was in the kitchen carrying the huge turkey from the refrigerator to the sink. "Isn't it beginning to seem like Thanksgiving?" she asked as if nothing in the world was wrong.

Ginger turned away blindly. "I guess so."

Mom said, "I saw Mrs. Lindberg at the market today, and she looked so frail and unhappy. Oh, Ginger, I hope you don't mind, but I invited her and Robin for Thanksgiving dinner tomorrow. We couldn't let them eat alone. Besides, we're only having Gram . . . and maybe your dad."

To Ginger's horror, tears burst to her eyes.

"Oh, dear . . ." Mom said, "I should have asked you."

Ginger shook her head wretchedly.

"What's wrong, Gin-ger?" Lilabet asked, her brown eyes wide with sympathy.

"Nothing . . . just nothing!" How could she say that Aunt Alice was dying . . . that she couldn't stand Robin Lindberg one more instant . . . and that everything was worse than anyone could even imagine!

Mom and Lilabet were staring at her, so Ginger added, "Anyhow, I feel terrible!" And with that, she tore off for her bedroom.

9

When Ginger opened her draperies on Thanksgiving morning, her spirits lifted. Sunshine streamed through the dark rain clouds, turning the sky into a dramatic sight. After such a rainy week she couldn't help hoping for another special ray of sunshine: that Aunt Alice would be fine.

Gathering up her courage, she headed for the hall phone to call Katie. *Lord, let things be all right,* she prayed.

Katie answered cheerfully. "Happy Thanksgiving!"

Encouraged, Ginger returned the greeting and asked, "How's Aunt Alice today?"

"Fine again," Katie answered, sounding relieved.

"The doctor gave her new pills. She surely is brave, isn't she?"

"She sure is," Ginger replied.

"You are, too," Katie said. "When we rode home from school yesterday, I saw inside Robin's hat. Something was erased under her name . . . probably *your* name! Anyhow, I didn't think about it till we dropped you off yesterday."

"I figured that's what happened," Ginger said.

"I feel sorry for her, but it wasn't right for her to steal your hat and ruin your soliloquy. I surely do think Miss Nordstrom should know when she returns!"

"I'd rather forget about it," Ginger decided.

"You sure?" Katie asked.

"Yeah. Thanks anyhow."

"Then I'll change the subject. What are you doing today?"

"Don't laugh, but we're having Robin and Mrs. Lindberg here for Thanksgiving dinner . . . and Gram and maybe Dad."

"Your dad, too?"

"Yeah . . . another of Mom's good-but-bad ideas."

After a long silence Katie said, "I'll pray for y'all to have a good Thanksgiving."

"Thanks." They'd never discussed praying, but now she admitted, "Yesterday I prayed for Aunt Alice to be out of pain."

"Me, too," Katie replied. "I wanted her to be all

right today, because her cousins are coming to visit. I'm so glad she's here. Without her, we'd be lonely for the rest of our family in Georgia."

When they hung up, Ginger thought about how good her friend was at counting her blessings, and she decided to count her own. First, having Katie for a friend . . . then, living with the Gabriels, Mom's happiness, going to Santa Rosita Christian, having a turkey and all the trimmings. Mom had even finished stenciling the flowers and ivy around the kitchen ceiling in time for Thanksgiving.

As the hours flew and the smell of roasting turkey wafted through the house, it appeared that Katie's prayers were answered. Even Joshua was pleasant to Ginger as they set the dining room table. She remarked, "Doesn't it look beautiful?"

He answered, "It's all right."

The table, covered with a lace tablecloth, was lengthened to seat ten people: six of them, including Grandfather, plus Gram, Dad, Robin, and Mrs. Lindberg. A cornucopia with apples, oranges, bananas, grapes, and nuts brightened the table. China, silverware, and goblets gleamed all around.

Grandfather went to pick up Mrs. Lindberg and Robin, then escorted them into the house. As they settled in the living room, he said to Grant, "Mrs. Lindberg tells me she'll be returning to my old church this Sunday. She and her late husband used to be regulars there. They provided great encouragement for me."

Mrs. Lindberg's voice was quieter than usual as she explained to Grant, "The new pastor might be different from your father, but I've decided to give him another try. I have a new hearing aid now, so I can hear. I can hear Robin better, too."

Robin gave Ginger a slight smile.

Mom called from the kitchen, "Gram and your father have just driven up, Ginger. Why don't you greet them at the door?"

Ginger chewed her gum hard. Probably Dad was still mad at her for going to Santa Rosita Christian. There was bound to be trouble if he spent the day with them. She opened the door.

Gram smiled hopefully over the mincemeat pie she'd brought for dinner. Dad stood behind her, his smile flashing beneath his thick, dark moustache. He wore an expensive camel-colored sports coat and dark brown slacks, and his kinky dark hair curled damply, like it was still wet from the shower.

"Hi," Ginger said to them. "Happy Thanksgiving."

Gram returned the greeting, but Ginger's attention went to her father.

"Happy Thanksgiving, kiddo," he said. He handed her a box wrapped in gold-covered foil. "Chocolates for you. Sweets for the sweet and all that."

"Thanks."

His brown eyes met hers. "I haven't seen you for a while. You doing okay?"

A while! It's been over two months! Ginger wanted to exclaim. Instead she cracked her gum and said, "Yeah, I'm okay."

"Good," he replied, "that's what Gram tells me. She keeps me up-to-date." His eyes moved to the gift-wrapped box between them. "I can't stay, but I'll pick Gram up at seven o'clock. I have other plans. Guess I should have let you know sooner."

"I'll tell Mom," Ginger replied, relieved. "Thanks for the chocolates."

Grinning, he nodded. "Sure, kiddo. I'd give you a knuckle rub if your hair didn't look so nice."

She smiled, knowing her red curls were probably as tangled as ever. "Yeah, I bet you would."

"See you, kiddo." Turning, he took off toward the driveway to his sports car.

Gram shook her head hopelessly, and Ginger shrugged.

"You're doing better," Gram said.

"Maybe a little," Ginger decided. At least Dad's fading out of her life didn't hurt quite so much now.

"I'm doing better, too," Gram said. "Ummm . . . it smells like turkey and dressing and yams cooking."

"It is," Ginger replied, closing the door behind Gram. "I'll take Dad's place setting off the table."

As they walked into the living room to join the others, Ginger noticed that Robin was watching them. She followed Ginger into the dining room.

"Your father's even more handsome than his picture," she remarked.

Ginger nodded. "Yeah, I guess he is."

"He's more handsome than Grant," Robin said.

Ginger heard her dad's car roar away. "You think so?"

"Lots more handsome," Robin said. "He could be a TV star or in the movies."

"I guess that kind of stuff isn't so important to me now," Ginger said. "Aunt Alice says, 'Handsome is as handsome does.' "

"What's that supposed to mean?"

Ginger didn't like to compare Dad and Grant, but she tried to explain. "I guess it means . . . the handsomest person is the one who's there to help you when you really need it."

Robin frowned in confusion.

"You know, someone who's responsible." Ginger turned away. "Excuse me, please, I have to go to the kitchen."

In the kitchen she told Mom, "Dad won't be eating here after all."

"That's too bad," Mom said, though she looked relieved, too.

When they all sat down for the sumptuous turkey dinner, Grant began with the very psalm Ginger had read to Aunt Alice, about entering God's gates with thanksgiving and His courts with praise. Then Grant started the "I'm-gratefuls" with, "Heavenly Father, I'm so grateful for this blended family and for how You help us to grow in love. Today especially my soul is so full of joy. Thank You, thank You!"

Mom said, "Lord, I'm so grateful . . . so very grateful for this happy home You've given us. Thank You for the song You've put in my heart. I do enter Your gates with wondrous thanksgiving and Your courts with praise!"

Ginger's heart felt a surge of gratefulness and it grew as she prayed, "Thank You, God, for this first Thanksgiving since I met You. Thank You for making my life so much better. Thank You for . . . Dad and for . . . Grant and Mom, Joshua and Lilabet, and for Gram and Mrs. Lindberg and Robin . . . and for the turkey and all the trimmings."

Joshua said, "Thank You, God, for giving us a new mother . . . and thank You for Ginger, too."

Ginger almost laughed, but Lilabet piped up, "Thank You, God, for Jesus!"

Grandfather waited for others, but Gram wasn't used to praying out loud and maybe Mrs. Lindberg wasn't either. Robin didn't say a thing. Grandfather added his eloquent thanks and concluded with, "And all of God's people said—"

"Amen," Ginger intoned with her family.

Grandfather said, "Leave it to the youngest to give our most important thanks: Thank You for Jesus. That was just the right thing to say, Lilabet."

Sitting on her booster chair, Lilabet beamed.

Robin hadn't said a thing, but Ginger's heart still brimmed so with gratefulness that she wasn't going to let anyone or anything spoil this Thanksgiving. She smiled at Robin.

"I'm hungry!" Lilabet said, "Let's eat!"

The next Wednesday, Aunt Alice looked as bright as the potted chrysanthemums still blooming in her bedroom. "How was your Thanksgiving, Ginger?" she asked.

"Just about perfect, except for eating too much," Ginger responded. "Even Robin didn't steal anything."

Aunt Alice smiled wryly. "It does seem a step in the right direction. I'm going to continue praying for both of you." She smiled at her. "Ready for reading a psalm or *The Wind in the Willows*?"

"Sure," Ginger answered. "I guess I'd like a Psalm first. I like reading them to you."

"I'm glad to hear you still do."

"And I still can't get over it," Ginger marveled. "It's just like I hoped."

Aunt Alice beamed. "God often gives us the desires of our hearts."

Ginger reached for the Bible. "Like my wanting to make money for Christmas presents for my family, then getting this job. Between my allowance and working here, I feel rich."

Aunt Alice laughed. "It is time to get started on presents, isn't it? It's fortunate that I can shop by phone. That reminds me, would you hand me the telephone directory before you leave?"

The next Wednesday Aunt Alice felt fine again.

Ginger noticed her "elephant picture," framed, on Aunt Alice's nightstand.

"I can't tell you how much I've enjoyed that picture—and our friendship," Aunt Alice said as Ginger sat down beside the bed. "And now I'm going to ask a great favor of you."

"What?" Ginger asked.

"I'm asking you not to grieve when I die."

Ginger felt her mouth drop open.

Aunt Alice smiled. "I'm sorry to take you so by surprise, but I think it's important to discuss death sometimes. Since you've been spending time with me, I think it's especially important that I discuss it with you."

"Aren't you . . . aren't you scared?" Ginger asked.

Aunt Alice's blue eyes glowed with joy as she slowly shook her head. "I've trusted God with so many other things, and He's never let me down. When my body dies, it's only an instant in time, then my spirit will be with Him. I won't be sick anymore . . . I'll be able to get around again. Maybe even run like the wind! And I already have many friends waiting for me with Him. I can't imagine anything more glorious. Can you?"

"I guess not. You make it sound wonderful."

"The Bible tells us that's how it can be," Aunt Alice said. "What bothers me is people like Robin who don't know the Lord . . . especially those who don't even want to know Him. Their separation

107

from God lasts forever. It's no wonder that so many people don't want to hear about death."

"I used to be really scared to think about it," Ginger admitted. "Now I guess it seems . . . more interesting."

"That's because you know the Lord," Aunt Alice said, "and you've put the number of your earthly days in His hands." She smiled. "Well, enough of that. What do you think Katie would like for Christmas?"

Ginger sat back with relief. "Maybe an angel. She likes my angel collection."

Aunt Alice said, "Please hand me that phone directory again when you leave."

By the middle of December, Christmas preparations at home were well under way. Ginger had figured out what to give everyone except Aunt Alice, who already had three poinsettias and a tiny Christmas tree in her bedroom. Finally Ginger asked her, "What would you like for Christmas?"

"I truly can't think of a thing," Aunt Alice said, "except maybe a Bible like yours."

"A kids' Bible?" Ginger asked.

Aunt Alice nodded. "For you to give to someone special."

"Who?" Ginger asked.

Aunt Alice said, "The Lord will let you know."

"But I want to give *you* something special," Ginger protested.

Aunt Alice's blue eyes met hers. "I know you do, Ginger. It would truly be the most special thing you could give."

Ginger wasn't so sure about that, but she decided not to press the matter. It would be crazy to give Aunt Alice a kids' Bible.

10

Aunt Alice was still on Ginger's mind Saturday morning when Grant took all of them to a Christmas tree farm to choose their tree. They decided on Ginger's favorite, a tall, full fir. Returning home with the tree tied to the roof of the car, they sang "Jingle Bells," even though the day was warm and bright with sunshine.

They returned in time for lunch, and Ginger gobbled her steaming chili and hot, buttered corn bread with the rest of them. "Can we decorate the tree right away?" she asked.

"It's time for Lilabet to have her nap," Mom said.

"I wanna help!" Lilabet yelled.

"We won't decorate the tree until after your nap,"

Grant assured her. "Joshua and I will only set it up in its stand, and we'll bring the boxes of ornaments into the living room. The faster you get to sleep, the sooner we can decorate the tree. Now you have a good nap so you're not grouchy."

"Okay," Lilabet agreed reluctantly. As Mom followed her down the hallway, she called back, "You wait for me!"

"We will," Grant promised again.

He asked Ginger, "How about helping Joshua and me bring in the ornaments from the garage? There's plenty that Lilabet won't mind our doing, like tying the big red plastic bow on the outdoor lantern and putting up the wreaths. We can put the star up on the roof, too."

"This is the best Christmas of my life," Ginger said.

"I'm glad," Grant replied, hugging her around the shoulders as they trooped out to the garage.

Joshua said, "Here comes Grandfather to help!"

Grandfather Gabriel was carrying a cardboard carton from the guest house. "I thought you might like to use my old olive wood creche on the mantel again this year."

"It wouldn't be a proper Christmas without it," Grant answered. "Why don't you tell Ginger where you bought it?"

"Where?" Ginger asked him.

"In Bethlehem at a shop that overlooks the Shepherds' Fields," Grandfather answered.

111

"In Bethlehem? You mean the real Bethlehem?"

He laughed. "Yes, indeed. And by the very fields where people think the angels sang the first noel to some very surprised shepherds."

Ginger remembered: *The first noel, the angels did say, was to certain poor shepherds in fields as they lay*. . . . She asked, "What does it look like there?"

Grandfather smiled at the memory. "The hills and fields are still home to shepherds and their sheep. There's no city on the fields, no suburbs or other developments. It's as it must have been when the great star hung above the stable and the angels surprised those shepherds. It's quite wonderful."

Ginger could almost picture it herself. "May I help you put the creche on the mantel?"

"I was hoping you would," he answered. "Let's cut some pine boughs in the yard to put underneath it. They soften the effect, just as the straw in the manger under our Lord softened His bed."

Together, Grandfather and Ginger cut the pine boughs and arranged them on the living room mantelpiece, then placed the olive wood creche and small figures: the babe, Mary, Joseph, the shepherds, and the animals. As they spoke of the first Christmas Eve, Ginger said, "I wish Aunt Alice could be here with us. Last week she talked about . . . about, you know, dying."

"Oh?" Grandfather replied.

Ginger nodded. "She's not scared."

Grandfather said, "I know. She's already discussed her memorial service with me."

By mid-afternoon, the huge star rose high over the roof, ready to be lighted at night. Inside, the house began to resemble a Christmas card scene. Mom had placed red and green candles among pine boughs on tables, and Ginger's fingers were sticky and black with pine tar, but it was worth it. Everything smelled piney like Christmas, and wreaths and ornaments decorated every room.

Lilabet arrived, blinking sleepily. "Did you dec'rate the tree?"

"Of course not," Mom said. "We've been waiting for you. How about some Christmas cookies for all of us, first? We have some misshapen gingerbread men who aren't going to make it onto the tree."

"*Ginger*bread cookies," Joshua teased.

"Never mind," Ginger said with a grin. She wasn't going to let any teasing—not even ginger teasing—bother her now. Not with Christmas in the air and all around them.

Grant put Christmas records on the stereo, and the sounds of carols and silvery bells filled the house as they all opened cartons and unwrapped the old-fashioned tree ornaments. By dinnertime, the tree was covered with ornaments, ropes of popcorn, gingerbread men, red velvety bows, and candy canes. A lighted angel topped the tree. At last they turned on the tiny white candlelike lights, and Ginger said, "It's the most beautiful tree I've ever seen. Even if you did have to put some *ginger*bread men on it."

After dinner, when they went out caroling with Katie's family, they lighted the star on the roof of the house, brightening the night sky. Ginger looked up at the stars and thought, *Thank You, Lord, for the real stars and the moon and the earth. And thank You most of all for Jesus and my new life this Christmas.*

As they started for school Wednesday morning, Grant said, "Katie won't be attending school today. They've had to get the doctor again for Aunt Alice. I doubt that you'll be working for her this afternoon, Ginger."

Ginger's heart sank. Aunt Alice was dying. It didn't seem fair, not now with everything decorated for Christmas and carols filling the air. Outside, the weather was warm and sunny. If Aunt Alice was dying today, you'd think that the skies would be pouring down rain like they had before Thanksgiving.

Late in the afternoon Miss Nordstrom stood before the class. She said in a solemn voice, "You'll remember that we've prayed for Katie's Great-Aunt Alice several times. This morning, her spirit passed on to be with the Lord."

Tears burst from Ginger's eyes, and she dug a tissue from her desk while everyone sat in silence.

After a moment, the kids buzzed with talk. At the

next desk, Robin said, "You don't have to make a big deal about it just because you knew her. She was just an old lady anyhow."

"Just an old lady anyhow!" Ginger repeated, appalled. "Aunt Alice, like the rest of us, was praying for you, Robin Lindberg. Not that you'd care about her or anyone else." Her tears made a blur of the room.

Miss Nordstrom said, "Let's all pray for Katie and her family now . . . and for Ginger, who was a special friend of Katie's Great-Aunt Alice in these last months, too."

Katie was absent on Thursday and Friday. Grant said the Camerons were making arrangements and getting ready for Aunt Alice's memorial service on Saturday afternoon—Christmas Eve Day! Ginger's heart hurt, as though it were squeezed in her chest. Aunt Alice had asked her not to grieve, but how could she help it?

She tried not to be sad as her class sang carols for the school's chapel program Friday afternoon. She caught Robin's glances at her. Probably Robin couldn't understand why anyone would be sad over "just an old lady."

Friday after school, Grandfather Gabriel took Ginger Christmas shopping. She bought plants for the kitchen for Mom, for Grant's office, for Gram's living room, and for Grandfather Gabriel's guest house, though he didn't know it. She bought an ocean book for Dad, a plane model for Joshua, and a beautiful seashell for Lilabet.

Grandfather helped her put everything in the trunk of his car. "All done?" he asked.

"Can we go to the Christian bookstore?" she asked.

"What for?" he inquired. "Or shouldn't I ask?"

"To get a book for Katie," she answered, not telling the whole truth. Crazy or not, she was going to buy the kids' Bible for Aunt Alice, too. Maybe Aunt Alice would know somehow. Ginger turned away quickly and gave her gum a crack.

When she awakened on Christmas Eve morning, her first thought was a downhearted, *Aunt Alice is dead. She won't be here for Christmas or next week or ever again.*

Mid-morning in the kitchen, Ginger helped Mom peel potatoes to take to the Camerons' house after the memorial service.

"I'm glad I gave up the soccer games to be with Aunt Alice," Ginger decided. "I can always play soccer, but maybe I'll never meet another person like Aunt Alice."

"Very likely you won't," Mom agreed, sad herself. "It was a privilege for our family to know her. I think even Lilabet and Raffles sensed that."

"Robin Lindberg said Aunt Alice was just an old lady."

Mom replied, "We'll have to continue to pray for Robin." She added, "I wonder what the surprise is that Grandfather arranged for the memorial service."

Ginger had never attended a memorial service, and she wasn't really looking forward to it, surprise or not. Grandfather would perform the service in his old church, and Joshua, who'd never met Aunt Alice, would stay home with Lilabet while she napped.

After lunch, Ginger dressed in the dark green plaid dress Gram had made her for Christmas and rode to the church with Mom and Grant. As they parked in the church lot, the palms of her hands were damp with nervousness.

"Look at all the cars," Mom said.

"The choir is probably practicing for the Christmas Eve service tonight," Grant said. He glanced at his watch. "We'd better get moving." He must have noticed how nervous Ginger felt as they hurried to the tan stucco church, for he patted her shoulder reassuringly.

Inside, quiet organ music filled the formal sanctuary, and sunlight streamed through the stained-glass windows. Masses of red poinsettias surrounded the choir loft and pulpit area, and white candles with red velvet ribbons rose from the pews along the aisles. Ginger followed Mom and Dad up the middle aisle, reflecting that even such a beautiful place couldn't stop the hurt in her heart.

She sat down between Mom and Grant in the third pew from the front. There were only a few people scattered around them. They settled back to listen to the music.

Before long, Katie's parents walked up the aisle with Katie and her brothers and Aunt Alice's cousins from Los Angeles. They looked sad, yet strong. Grandfather followed all of them, dignified in his black robe. When they reached the front of the sanctuary, he seated them in the first pew, then went up to the pulpit.

He sat down until the quiet organ music ended and the sanctuary was perfectly silent, then he stepped solemnly to the pulpit. "We are gathered here to honor the memory of a special lady, Alice Cameron," he began. "Most of Alice's friends have already passed on, and only the few of us here had the special privilege of knowing her."

Ginger pressed her quivering lips together. She must not grieve . . . she *must not* for Aunt Alice's sake!

Grandfather said, "Alice Cameron loved the Lord so much that her joy was evident. It bubbled over and blessed us, turning even her final days into a celebration. How fitting for her to die during the Christmas season when we celebrate the birth of our Savior."

His voice deepened. "Christ told us, 'In my Father's house are many rooms; if it were not so, I would have told you. I am going there to prepare a place for you.' Christ also said, 'You know the way to the place where I am going. I am the way and the

118

truth and the life. No one comes to the Father except through me.' "

Grandfather smiled so joyously that Ginger's heart hurt a bit less. He asked, "How do we know she is with Him?" Then he answered, "The Lord said, 'I am the resurrection and the life. He who believes in me will live, even though He dies, and whoever lives and believes in me will never die.' "

He spoke of God's promises to believers and read Psalm 100, Aunt Alice's favorite. Ginger remembered snatches of it: "Shout for joy to the Lord, all the earth. Worship the Lord with gladness, come before him with joyful songs. . . . Enter his gates with thanksgiving and his courts with praise. . . ."

"Alice Cameron asked me to have a joyous service," he said. "Instead of grieving, she wanted us to turn our minds to Christ, whom she so loved. The Lord has surely given her the desire of her heart, for we have a special treat. The choir is practicing for tonight's Christmas Eve service, and they will celebrate Christ's life and Alice Cameron's life by singing 'The Hallelujah Chorus' for us."

He paused, then gazed upward with joy and proclaimed, "Christ lives . . . hallelujah! Praise ye the Lord . . . hallelujah!"

The organ burst forth and everyone rose to their feet as the choir filed in, singing with exultation, "*Hal*—le-lu-jah! *Hal*—le-lu-jah! Hal-le-lu-jah Hal-le-lu-jah! Hal-*le-lu*-jah!"

Shivers rushed through Ginger's body as the

jubilant hallelujahs were repeated. "For the Lord God omnipotent reigneth . . . The Kingdom of this world is become the kingdom of our Lord and of His Christ! . . . King of kings, and Lord of lords . . . And He shall reign forever and ever . . . forever and ever, forever and ever."

While the magestic hallelujahs and forever-and-evers echoed and reechoed through the sanctuary, Ginger's spirit soared. Aunt Alice was with Jesus. She was! She was! Tears of joy rolled down Ginger's cheeks.

Later, at Katie's house, everyone talked about how much Aunt Alice had loved the Lord. They weren't grieving, Ginger realized. Instead, they'd fixed their thoughts on Jesus, just as Aunt Alice had wished.

That night during her own church's Christmas Eve service, right in the midst of singing "Joy to the World," Ginger prayed, *Thank You, Lord, that Aunt Alice is out of pain and with You.* To her surprise, she really and truly meant it.

When they returned home, Grant and Mom hurried into the living room to turn on the tiny white candle tree lights and put on Christmas records. "Okay, kids, you can come in," Grant announced.

"Deck the Halls" filled the house, and the room smelled of pine and bay candles. Ginger's eyes went to the shimmering Christmas tree and, under it, the gifts.

Ahead of her, Lilabet pointed at the fireplace hearth. "Look at the big angel!" she marveled.

Ginger stared. A wondrous angel doll as tall as she was stood on the hearth; she wore a white lace gown, silvery gossamer wings, and a halo on her golden curls. The angel hadn't been there before church. Maybe Grandfather put her there.

Grant handed a card to her. "It's for Ginger."

"For me?!" Ginger said. She looked at the unfamiliar handwriting on the envelope. *To Ginger, my earthly guardian angel.* Her eyes flew to the signature. "From Aunt Alice!" she cried. She blinked hard before she could read the other words. *Thank you for being my earthly guardian angel. I wanted you and Katie to have these twin angels for all of your Christmases, so you'd remember how much I treasured your friendship. Love, Aunt Alice.*

Grandfather said, "There are two other packages for you from Alice Cameron."

"Two more?" Ginger asked, still overwhelmed by the angel.

"Go ahead and open them," Mom said, "these are special. We can wait to open our gifts for a few minutes."

Recognizing Aunt Alice's spidery script on the package Mom handed her, Ginger tore open the red-and-white wrapping paper and opened the box. "A soccer ball?!"

Aunt Alice had written on a card, *Katie told me how you sacrificed your soccer games to keep your promise to me. I've appreciated it more than words can say, and I'm sure the Lord is pleased that you keep your word. May you now play soccer to your heart's content!*

Ginger blinked hard again, hoping she wouldn't bawl.

Grant handed her another package. "Here's the last one."

To Ginger, the world's greatest mahout, the card said. She opened the box and pulled aside the tissue paper. "A wooden elephant. It's because . . . she and I both rode elephants."

"Oh, my—" Mom said, "I think I might cry myself."

"Aunt Alice was a very special person," Grandfather said.

Ginger blinked hard again. "She sure was."

Later, when everyone was busily opening presents, a knock sounded at the front door.

"Maybe it's Santa Claus!" Lilabet called out.

"I doubt that," Grant laughed as he headed for the door.

For an instant, Ginger thought it might be her father, but he was taking her and Gram out for dinner on New Year's Day.

Grant returned to the living room. "Ginger, it's Robin Lindberg. She won't come in, but she has something for you."

A present? Ginger wondered. She didn't have anything to give Robin, not unless. . . . Scarcely

122

thinking, she grabbed a book from under the tree and hurried to the door.

Robin stood outside, holding a bag. She wore her old dark blue coat, but even wearing it and with the darkness of night behind her, she looked almost cheerful—like a Robin should.

"Hi," she said shyly. "I—I brought you something."

"Thanks," Ginger replied. "Why don't you come in? It's a little cold out there."

Robin shook her head, still holding the bag.

Ginger asked, "You want me to open it now?"

"Later," Robin answered. "Besides, it's not a present."

"Oh." They stared at each other for a long time, and Ginger finally asked, "Are you having a nice Christmas?"

Robin nodded, her blue eyes sparkling. "That's why I brought this. You—you and your family were kind to me, no matter how nasty I was—" Her voice shook, but she continued. "I—I saw you through the window the day you brought the India doll . . . so I knew you realized I stole the other one—"

"You saw me?" Ginger asked.

Robin nodded guiltily. "I'm really sorry. I—I brought both dolls back to you."

"Aw . . . no, Robin," Ginger said, still awkwardly holding the book behind her. "You keep them. Besides, I don't play much with dolls."

Robin placed the bag on the entry floor determinedly. "I have to give them to you. They'd always remind me of how awful I've been. Anyhow, I went to church with my great-gram tonight and they sang 'Silent Night' and 'The Hallelujah Chorus' and everything and . . . I decided. I—I wanted to be like you."

"You wanted to be like me!" Ginger repeated.

"You know, caring about old ladies and honest and stuff," Robin answered. "Anyhow, something happened, and I'm not scared or mad anymore. I'm a . . . Christian now, too."

"You're a Christian!"

Robin nodded again. "I got tired of acting . . . pretending. I wanted to be . . . you know—my real self."

"Yeah, I do know!" Ginger said, growing more and more excited. "But I have to tell you, Robin, Aunt Alice was the one who got the India doll for you, and we were praying for you . . . and . . . oh, Robin, I'm so glad!"

She wanted to throw her arms around Robin, but her hands still held the book behind her. She knew now why she'd bought the book. Aunt Alice had said the Lord would help her know what to do with it—and now she did.

"Here. It's a present for you." Ginger thrust the unwrapped kids' Bible that Aunt Alice had asked for toward Robin. "I know it sounds weird, but I think God wants me to give this to you."

"A Bible?" Robin gazed from it to Ginger.

"A kids' Bible with pictures, just like mine," Ginger said.

She remembered something she'd learned in Sunday school. "You're my sister now, Robin. All Christians are like sisters and brothers in the Lord."

Robin stared at her and suddenly, without thinking, Ginger pulled her out of the darkness and into the light in the house. To her amazement, they were hugging and laughing, hot tears rolling down their cheeks.

Ginger wanted to laugh and cry. Her heart thundered with such excitement, it seemed the hallelujahs from Aunt Alice's memorial service echoed in the air around them. "Now it's really the best Christmas of my life!" she exulted. She wiped her tears and her nose. "Come tell everyone else, Robin."

Robin's dark blue eyes filled with alarm. "But I've been so awful—"

"You're just like I was last summer. And you know what? They'll love you!"

"They will?"

In the living room, music rang out from the stereo. "Joy to the world, the Lord is come. . . ."

Ginger slipped an arm around Robin's shoulder. "Yeah," she promised. "Come on. They'll love you anyhow!"

HERE COMES GINGER!

God, stop Mom's wedding!

Ginger's world is falling apart. Her mom has recently become a Christian and, even worse, has fallen in love with Grant Gabriel. Ginger can't stand the thought of leaving their little house near the beach . . . moving in with Grant and his two children . . . trading in her "brown cave of a bedroom" for a yellow canopied bed.

Ginger tries to fight the changes she knows are coming—green fingernails, salt in the sugar bowl, a near disaster at the beach. But she finds that change can happen inside her, too, when she meets the Lord her mom has come to trust.

The Ginger Series
Here Comes Ginger!	A Job for an Angel
Off to a New Start	Absolutely Green

ELAINE L. SCHULTE is a southern Californian, like Ginger. She has written many stories, articles, and books for all ages, but the **Ginger Trumbell Books** is her first series for kids.

Chariot Books™
David C. Cook Publishing Co.

OFF TO A NEW START

Aoooouuuuh!
Aoooooouuuuuh!

The blast of Ginger's conch shell sounds through the Gabriels' house. But is it a call to battle or a plea for peace?

Some days Ginger isn't sure, as she struggles to find her place in her new "combined" family, in her new school, and as a new child of God. With the wise counsel of Grandfather Gabriel and the support of her family, Ginger learns some important lessons about making friends and making peace.

The Ginger Series

Here Comes Ginger!   A Job for an Angel
Off to a New Start   Absolutely Green

ELAINE L. SCHULTE is a southern Californian, like Ginger. She has written many stories, articles, and books for all ages, but the **Ginger Trumbell Books** is her first series for kids.

Chariot Books™
David C. Cook Publishing Co.

ABSOLUTELY GREEN

Green with envy—that's Ginger!

Life with her new "combined family" has just begun to feel natural when Ginger's mom and stepdad make an announcement: a new baby is on the way!

They sure are happy about it, but Ginger doesn't know what to think. It's clear that her stepbrother, Joshua, is anything but pleased—and for some reason, the news seems to make him grouchier than ever with Ginger.

Together Ginger's family discovers how God's love can conquer even feelings of resentment and jealousy.

The Ginger Series
Here Comes Ginger!   A Job for an Angel
Off to a New Start   Absolutely Green

ELAINE L. SCHULTE is a southern Californian, like Ginger. She has written many stories, articles, and books for all ages, but the **Ginger Trumbell Books** is her first series for kids.

Chariot Books™
David C. Cook Publishing Co.